Using the
Next Generation
Science
Standards
With Gifted and
Advanced Learners

Using the
Next Generation
Science
Standards
With Gifted and
Advanced Learners

Cheryll M. Adams, Ph.D.,
Alicia Cotabish, Ed.D.,
and Mary Cay Ricci

A Service Publication of the

PRUFROCK PRESS INC.
WACO, TEXAS

Library of Congress Cataloging-in-Publication Data

Adams, Cheryll M., 1948-
Using the next generation science standards with gifted and advanced learners : a
service publication of the Ntional Association for Gifted Children / by Cheryll M.
Adams,Ph.D.,Alicia Cotabish,Ed.D.,and Mary Cay Ricci.
    pages cm
Includes bibliographical references.
ISBN 978-1-61821-106-4 (pbk.)
1. Science--Study and teaching--United States. 2. Science--Study and teaching--Stan-
dards--United States. 3. Gifted children--Education--United States. 4. Gifted chil-
dren--Identification. I. Title.
Q183.3.A1A34 2013
371.95'3350973--dc23
                                    2013023328

Edited by Rachel Taliaferro

Production design by Raquel Trevino

ISBN-13: 978-1-61821-106-4

At the time of this book's publication, all facts and figures cited are the most current available. All telephone numbers, addresses, and website URLs are accurate and active. All publications, organizations, websites, and other resources exist as described in the book, and
all have been verified. The authors and Prufrock Press Inc. make no warranty or guarantee
concerning the information and materials given out by organizations or content found at
websites, and we are not responsible for any changes that occur after this book's publication.
If you find an error, please contact Prufrock Press Inc.

Prufrock Press Inc.
P.O. Box 8813
Waco, TX 76714-8813
Phone: (800) 998-2208
Fax: (800) 240-0333
http://www.prufrock.com

Table of Contents

Acknowledgments   vii

Foreword   ix

Preface   xi

Introduction   xvi

Alignment of the NGSS With Other Standards   1

Linking the NGSS to the CCSS in Math
    and English Language Arts   7

Finding and Developing Talent With NGSS
    and Gifted Education Strategies   10

Developing Innovative and Creative Scientists   13

Sample Learning Experiences for Advanced
    and Gifted Students in Science   21

Differentiating Assessments to Encourage
    Higher Level Reasoning   53

Talent Trajectory: Creating Pathways to Excellence in Science   58

Implementing the NGSS With Various
    Program Models in Gifted Education   63

Implications for Professional Learning When
    Implementing the NGSS   67

Collaboration to Support Achievement   72

A Possible Timeline for Locally Adapting
    the NGSS for Advanced Students   75

Resources to Assist With the Implementation Process   78

References   84

Appendix A: Definitions of Key Terms   90

Appendix B: Evidence-Based Practices in Gifted Education   94

Appendix C: Annotated References on Science and Giftedness   99

Appendix D: Additional Science Resources   105

About the Authors   109

Acknowledgments

Many people have assisted with the efforts in developing this book. They include the leadership of NAGC, the NAGC Professional Standards Committee, reviewers, NAGC staff, and experts who were a part of the development of the other books in this series on using the Common Core State Standards with gifted and advanced learners.

We would like to thank Paula Olszewski-Kubilius, NAGC president, and the NAGC Board, who have understood the urgency for responding to the national standards movement, including the Next Generation Science Standards (NGSS) and the Common Core State Standards (CCSS), and the gifted education community's need to have a voice in their implementation. From the beginning, the NAGC Professional Standards Committee also has been actively involved in providing the framework, expertise, and support for this book. Moreover, the NAGC leadership group also includes Nancy Green, Executive Director of the NAGC, and NAGC Association Editor Carolyn Callahan, who have supported the development process and the need for this book.

This book has also been strengthened through a rigorous review process. We want to thank these reviewers who took time to provide valuable advice and feedback: Debbie Dailey, Jeff Danielian, Jennifer Hoffman, Chrys Mursky, and Janice Robbins.

Finally, the authors want to express a special thank you to Jane Clarenbach, Director of Public Education at the NAGC office, who has provided the needed energy in supporting the authors through the process and a critical eye in editing the many drafts of this book. She has shepherded this writing project along with her many other duties with great diplomacy, tact, and endless amounts of patience.

Foreword

As soon as it was clear that the Common Core State Standards and, now, the Next Generation Science Standards (NGSS) were going to become the foundation for curriculum in many states, NAGC heard from the membership about the need for tools to apply the curriculum to high-ability learners. Earlier books addressed the Common Core State Standards. This book was created for those teachers who will be using the new science standards in their classrooms.

Gifted educators are excited that the NGSS reflect many of the strategies that the field of gifted education has been stressing for decades as important to deep learning, engagement, and high achievement—high-level, analytical thinking, advanced problem-solving skills, and cross-discipline connections. Although the NGSS are more rigorous than the current science standards found in many states, the NGSS will not ensure that gifted children receive the advanced content, accelerative options, and high-level enrichment that they need to be challenged and make continuous progress in science education. Hence this book, to help educators understand how to use the NGSS as a foundation, but also to go beyond them for those learners who meet the

standards earlier and faster, as the NGSS creators have acknowl-
edged some students will do. Our nation needs our best science
students to be challenged and supported in their studies starting
in the earliest grades.

This book also assists educators in coupling and integrating
the NGSS with gifted education curricula, instructional practices, and program models. It is a useful resource for all educators, not just those who specifically work in gifted programs. As
we know, most gifted children receive their instruction from
teachers in heterogeneous classrooms who may have little to no
training in the needs of gifted students and who need assistance in
differentiating content and instruction for high-ability learners.

Relying once again on a workgroup model, NAGC is
indebted to Cheryll Adams, Alicia Cotabish, and Mary Cay
Ricci, who responded quickly to review the draft standards,
provided input for NAGC comments to the NGSS developers,
and produced this valuable resource for teachers and curriculum
planners. I thank them for the many, many hours they invested
in this effort.

Paula Olszewski-Kubilius
NAGC President 2011–2013

Preface

The purpose of this book is to provide classroom teachers and administrators with examples and strategies to implement the new Next Generation Science Standards (NGSS) for advanced learners at all stages of development in K–12 schools. One aspect of fulfilling that purpose is to clarify what advanced opportunities look like for such learners from primary through secondary grade levels. Specifically, how is effective differentiation designed for high-ability learners in science? How can educators provide the appropriate level of rigor and relevance within the new standards as they translate them into experiences for gifted learners? How can educators provide creative and innovative opportunities to nurture the thinking, reasoning, problem solving, passion, and inventiveness of our best students in this subject area?

In this book, we will describe trajectories for talent development in science. These progressions lend vision to the work of teachers as they deliver classroom instruction at one level and prepare students for succeeding at higher levels in the journey toward self-fulfillment and the real world of science, technology, engineering, and mathematics (STEM) professions. What are the skills, habits of mind, and attitudes toward learning needed to reach high levels of competency and creative production in science fields? How does the pathway from novice to expert differ among promising learners?

The book also includes multiple resources in the appendices to support educators in developing and modifying materials for students who are advanced in science. In addition to including a list of definitions of the key terms used in this book (Appendix A), we have included a research base of best practices in gifted education (Appendix B), annotated references to key publications and websites focused on science and giftedness (Appendix C), and a list of publications addressing science and K–12 students (Appendix D).

The book is also based on a set of underlying assumptions about the constructs of giftedness and talent development that underpin the thinking that spawned this work. These assumptions are:

1. Giftedness is developed over time through the interaction of potential with nurturing environmental conditions. Thus, the process is developmental, dynamic, and malleable.

2. Many learners show preferences for particular subject matter early and continue to select learning opportunities that match their predispositions if they are provided with opportunities to do so. Thus, evidence of talent development emerges not only from work done in school but also from outside of school in cocurricular or extracurricular contexts.

3. Aptitudes and interests also may emerge as a result of exposure to high-level, engaging, and challenging activities. Thus, teachers should consider using advanced learning activities and techniques as a stimulus for all learners.

4. Intellectual, cultural, and learning diversity among learners may account for different rates of learning, different areas of aptitude, different cognitive styles, and different experiential backgrounds. Working with such diversity

in the classroom requires teachers to differentiate and customize curriculum and instruction, always working to provide an optimal match between the learner and her readiness to encounter the next level of challenge.

Users of this book need to be sensitive to the ideas contained herein as not intended to apply exclusively to identified gifted students—they also apply to students with potential in science, as they might develop motivation and readiness to learn within the domain of science.

Finally, it is our hope that the book provides a roadmap for meaningful national, state, and local educational reform that elevates learning in science to higher levels of passion, proficiency, and creativity for gifted and, indeed, all learners.

Rationale for the Work

The adoption of the NGSS is cause for gifted education as a field to reflect on its role in supporting gifted and high-potential learners appropriately in the content areas. The field of gifted education has not always differentiated systematically in the core domains of learning, but rather has focused on interdisciplinary concepts, higher level skills, and problem solving across domains. With the new NGSS and their national focus, it becomes critical to show how to differentiate for gifted learners within a set of standards that are reasonably rigorous in each domain.

NGSS and Gifted Learners

The authors of the NGSS acknowledge the unique needs of gifted learners (Achieve, Inc., 2013); however, it is reasonable to assume that general classroom teachers may limit themselves to the student performance expectations and clarification statements in the NGSS as they develop curriculum materials. Unfortunately, many of the statements and assessment boundaries found in the NGSS are limiting and could be interpreted as support for a "one size fits all" approach. Although the standards are strong, they are not sufficiently advanced to accommodate the needs of most learners who are gifted in science. And although the NGSS developers acknowledge that effective differentiation strategies such as accelerated pacing, increased challenge, opportunities for self-direction, and strategic grouping may be employed to meet the needs of advanced learners (Achieve, Inc., 2013), some students will traverse the standards before the end of high school, which will require educators to provide advanced content for them. In addition to accelerative methods, there is also a need to enrich and extend the standards by ensuring that there are open-ended opportunities to meet the standards through multiple pathways; more complex, creative, and innovative thinking applications; and real-world problem-solving contexts. This requires a deliberate strategy among gifted educators to ensure that the NGSS are translated in a way that allows for differentiated practices to be employed with gifted and high-potential students.

As with all standards, new assessments likely will drive the instructional process. As a field, gifted educators must be aware of the need to differentiate new assessments that align with the NGSS and content as well. Gifted learners will need to be assessed through performance-based and portfolio techniques that are based on higher level learning outcomes and may vary from the more traditional assessments the NGSS may employ.

Although the new NGSS appear to be a positive movement for all of education, it is important to be mindful of the ongoing need to differentiate appropriately for top learners. As a field, it is also critical to agree on the need to align with this work so gifted education's voices are at the table as the NGSS become one important basis, along with the newly revised InTASC Model Teacher Standards (Council of Chief State School Officers, 2011), for elevating teacher quality and student learning nationwide.

The Next Generation Science Standards have significant implications for teaching science in grades K–12. Our collective future lies in the individual development of students with science promise, students who will fulfill their own potential and also provide leadership for others. This individualized developmental approach includes students who traditionally have been identified as gifted, talented, advanced, or precocious in science, as well as those students of promise who may have been excluded from the rich opportunities that might accompany this recognition. As with all students, these students with special needs deserve a learning environment that lifts the ceiling, fuels their creativity and passions, pushes them to make continuous progress throughout their academic careers, and supports them in the fulfillment of their personal potential.

Introduction

The NGSS are standards for K–12 science education illustrating the curriculum emphases needed for students to develop scientific literacy required for college readiness and the 21st century. Based on the *Framework for K–12 Science Education* (National Research Council [NRC], 2012) and developed by experts across the disciplines of science, engineering, cognitive science, teaching and learning, curriculum, assessment, and education policy, the process of the NGSS's evolution considered the importance of having the scientific and educational research communities identify core ideas in science and articulate them across grade bands. In the development phase of the standards, 26 states provided leadership by addressing common issues involved in adoption and implementation of the standards. The initiative was coordinated by Achieve, Inc., a nonprofit bipartisan organization, and involved a range of networks including the 35-state American Diploma Project Network (ADPN) and the network of 24 states in the Partnership for Assessment of Readiness for College and Careers (PARCC). The state-led process of development included state policy leaders, higher education professors, K–12 teachers, and the science and business communities.

When navigating the standards, educators have two options to view the standards: by topical arrangement (much like the arrangement of most standards in education) or by disciplinary core ideas (i.e., physical science, life science, Earth and space science, engineering, technology, and applications of science). Furthermore, users can easily navigate the standards by topical arrangement or disciplinary core idea through an interactive filtering system available on the NGSS website.

Three Dimensions of the Next Generation Science Standards

The NGSS authors combined three dimensions of science to form each standard. The dimensions encompass a vision of what it means to be a scientist. Educators should be aware of the following dimensions as they plan to differentiate the standards.

- *Dimension 1: Science and Engineering Practices* describes behaviors of scientists, explains and extends what is meant by "inquiry" in science, and focuses on the knowledge beyond skills that are needed to engage in science.
- *Dimension 2: Crosscutting Concepts* cohesively links different domains of science that have application across domains. They include: patterns, similarity, and diversity; cause and effect; scale, proportion, and quantity; systems and system models; energy and matter; structure and functions; and stability and change.
- *Dimension 3: Disciplinary Core Ideas* (DCI) is grouped in four domains: the physical sciences, the life sciences, the Earth and space sciences, and engineering teaching and application of science. DCI are grounded in K–12 science curriculum, instruction, and assessment, and are considered to be the most important aspects in the teaching and learning of science. The DCI are shaped by ideas that have broad discipline importance, key organizing concepts, key features of understanding or investigating complex ideas in science, and student and societal

impact. The following sections provide more information about each.

Dimension 1: Scientific and Engineering Practices

When considering the implications of the NGSS for the development of science talent, it is important to take into account the eight standards for scientific and engineering practices that educators should seek to develop in their students, as well as the individual science content standards. According to the authors of the NGSS, practices describe behaviors that scientists engage in "as they investigate and build models and theories about the natural world and the key set of engineering practices that engineers use as they design and build models and systems" (Achieve, Inc, 2013b, para. 2). These scientific and engineering Practices are an integral part of the NGSS. These build on the National Research Council's *A Framework for K–12 Education* (2012), produced exclusively for the NGSS. The practices increase in complexity and sophistication across grade levels. These are the eight NGSS for scientific and engineering practices for all students from kindergarten through college and careers:

1. Asking questions (for science) and defining problems (for engineering)
2. Developing and using models
3. Planning and carrying out investigations
4. Analyzing and interpreting data
5. Mathematics and computational thinking
6. Construct explanations (for science) and design solutions (for engineering)
7. Engaging in argument in evidence
8. Obtain, evaluate, and communicate information

It is important that students actively engage in these practices daily in their science classes. Students need ongoing opportunities to experience the joy of investigating rich concepts in depth and applying reasoning and justification to a variety of scientific, engineering, and other problems.

In response to the release of the Common Core State Standards for Mathematics, Johnsen and Sheffield (2013) proposed a ninth standard focused on creativity and innovation. The authors of this book will follow suit and propose a ninth standard for scientific and engineering practice be added for the development of promising science students—a standard on scientific and engineering creativity and innovation:

1. *Solve problems in novel ways and pose new scientific questions of interest to investigate.*

The characteristics of the new proposed standard would be that students are encouraged and supported in taking risks, embracing challenge, solving problems in a variety of ways, posing new scientific questions of interest to investigate, and being passionate about scientific investigations.

Dimension 2: Crosscutting Concepts: An Integrated Approach

The NGSS crosscutting concepts are application-based concepts that cut across multiple domains of science. The crosscutting concepts are an organizational schema for interrelating knowledge and they represent a more integrated view of science learning. Specifically, the crosscutting concepts are:

1. patterns
2. cause and effect: mechanism and explanation
3. scale, proportion, and quantity
4. systems and system models
5. energy and matter: flow, cycle, and conservation
6. structure and function
7. stability and change

Crosscutting concepts are arranged in grade bands (grades K–2, grades 3–5, grades 6–8, and grades 9–12), which lessens ceiling effects. They represent conceptual characteristics of what scientists should be able to "do" and cut across multiple domains. For example, consider a task to explain the effect mass has on a falling object. It could be assessed using the grade band information described in the cause and effect: mechanisms and explanation concept. The expectation could be for students to use conceptual models (e.g., Newton's Second Law of Motion) in concert with a practice, such as modeling, to develop a structure or function (using different materials or components) to demonstrate the effects of mass on a falling object. Related tasks could be planning or carrying out investigations using mathematical and computational thinking, which are both part of the science and engineering practices. The tasks can be conducted over time to develop a portfolio of evidence about students' understandings and enactments of crosscutting concepts. For the gifted learner, advanced and complex tasks should be integrated to elevate learning.

Dimension 3: Disciplinary Core Ideas

Disciplinary core ideas (DCI) demonstrate a progression of ideas arranged in grade bands across four domains: the physical sciences, the life sciences, the Earth and space sciences, and engineering technology and applications of science. To be considered core in the NGSS, the ideas have to meet at least two of the following criteria:

1. Have broad importance across multiple sciences or engineering disciplines or be a key organizing concept of a single discipline.
2. Provide a key tool for understanding or investigating more complex ideas and solving problems.
3. Relate to the interests and life experiences of students or be connected to societal or personal concerns that require scientific or technological knowledge.
4. Be teachable and learnable over multiple grades at increasing levels of depth and sophistication.

The organization of the DCI into grade bands creates overlapping at times; however, the arrangement is conducive to an integrated approach to science learning and creates an accelerated trajectory for gifted learners. For example, Figure 1 demonstrates the expected increase in sophistication of student thinking as typical students progress through selected concepts of Earth and space science. However, advanced science students may accelerate through the progression more quickly. With the possibility of exhausting the progression model, high-ability secondary science students would need additional accommodations to eliminate possible ceiling effects.

INCREASING SOPHISTICATION OF STUDENT THINKING

	K–2	3–5	6–8	9–12
ESS1.A The universe and its stars	Patterns of movement of the sun, moon, and stars as seen from Earth can be observed, described, and predicted.	Stars range greatly in size and distance from Earth and this can explain their relative brightness.	The solar system is part of the Milky Way, which is one of many billions of galaxies.	Light spectra from stars are used to determine their characteristics, processes, and lifecycles. Solar activity creates the elements through nuclear fusion. The development of technologies has provided the astronomical data that provide the empirical evidence for the Big Bang theory.
ESS1.B Earth and the solar system		The Earth's orbit and rotation, and the orbit of the moon around the Earth cause observable patterns.	The solar system contains many varied objects held together by gravity. Solar system models explain and predict eclipses, lunar phases, and seasons.	Kepler's laws describe common features of the motions of orbiting objects. Observations from astronomy and space probes provide evidence for explanations of solar system formation. Changes in Earth's tilt and orbit cause climate changes such as Ice Ages.
ESS1.C The history of planet Earth	Some events on Earth occur very quickly; others can occur very slowly.	Certain features on Earth can be used to order events that have occurred in a landscape.	Rock strata and the fossil record can be used as evidence to organize the relative occurrence of major historical events in Earth's history.	The rock record resulting from tectonic and other geoscience processes as well as objects from the solar system can provide evidence of Earth's early history and the relative ages of major geologic formations.

Figure 1. Progressions within the Next Generation Science Standards. From *Next Generation Science Standards*, by Achieve, Inc., 2013a, Washington, DC: Achieve, Inc. Copyright 2013 by Achieve, Inc. Reprinted with permission.

Alignment of the NGSS
With Other Standards

All differentiation is based on an understanding of the characteristics of gifted and high-potential students *and* the content standards within a domain. The new NGSS provide an opportunity for the field of gifted education to examine its practices and align them more fully to the NAGC Pre-K–Grade 12 Gifted Programming Standards (2010) for curriculum, instruction, and assessment. For example, similar to the NAGC Programming Standards, which represent the professional standards for programs in gifted education across Pre-K–12 levels, the NGSS emphasize problem solving (NAGC, 2010) and the NGSS disciplinary core ideas spread across the four domains of (a) physical sciences, (b) life sciences, (c) Earth and space sciences, and (d) engineering, technology, and applications of sciences. Because the gifted programming standards in curriculum require educators to engage in two major tasks in curriculum planning—alignment to standards in the content areas and the development of a scope and sequence—using the NGSS is a natural point of departure. The effort must occur in vertical planning teams within districts and states in order to increase the likelihood of consistency and coherence in the process.

Within the gifted education programming standards, the curriculum and assessment standards were used to design the science book in the following ways:

- *Development of scope and sequence.* This book has demonstrated a set of interrelated emphases/activities for use across K–12 with a common format and within key content domains.
- *Use of differentiation strategies.* The book developers used the central differentiation strategies emphasized in the standards, including critical and creative thinking, problem solving, inquiry, research, and concept development.
- *Use of appropriate pacing/acceleration techniques, including preassessment, formative assessment, and pacing.* The book developers used all of these strategies, as well as more advanced, innovative, and complex science learning experiences to ensure the challenge level for gifted learners.
- *Adaptation or replacement of the core curriculum.* The project extends the NGSS by ensuring that advanced and gifted learners master them and then go beyond them in key ways. Some standards may be mastered earlier and the science and engineering practices should be used consistently throughout the curriculum.
- *Use of research-based materials.* The book developers have included models and techniques found to be highly effective with advanced and gifted learners in enhancing critical thinking, reasoning and sense-making, problem solving, and innovation. They have also used some of the techniques found in Project Clarion (http://education. wm.edu/centers/cfge/research/completed/clarion/ index.php), the Earth as a System is Essential Project (EaSiE; http://www.easie-mmsa.org/), and University of Iowa's PRISMS Plus (Cooney, Escalada, & Unruh, 2008). These are research-based science programs and resources that are used nationally and can be beneficial for advanced and gifted learners.

- *Use of information technologies.* The examples provided suggest the use of visual media, computer technology, and multimedia in the learning experiences developed for this book.
- *Use of metacognitive strategies.* The book developers included activities where students use reflection, planning, monitoring, and assessing skills.
- *Talent development in areas of aptitude and interest in various domains (e.g., cognitive, affective, aesthetic).* The book presents examples that provide multiple opportunities for students to explore domain-specific interests, such as conducting research, investigating problems, creating models, and exercising multiple levels of skills in cognitive, affective, and aesthetic areas.

21st Century Skills

This book also includes a major emphasis on key 21st century skills (Partnership for 21st Century Skills, n.d.) in overall orientation as well as in the instructional experiences and assessments employed in the examples. The National Science Teachers Association (NSTA) recognized the important connection between science education and 21st century skills. "Exemplary science education can offer a rich context for developing many 21st century skills, such as critical thinking, problem solving, and information literacy, especially when instruction addresses the nature of science and promotes use of science practices" (NSTA, 2011, para. 4). Through the exemplars presented in this book, students will consistently think critically, communicate ideas and findings, and collaborate on hypotheses, experiments, and data collection.

Although many 21st century skills are imbedded in the sample learning experiences for both the typical and advanced learner, all challenging science instruction should be supported by the following 21st century skills.

- *Collaboration*: Students are encouraged to work with partners and small groups to carry out tasks and projects, to pose and solve problems, and to plan presentations.
- *Communication*: Students are encouraged to develop communication skills in written, oral, visual, and technological modes in a balanced format within each unit of study.
- *Critical thinking*: Students are provided with models of critical thought that are incorporated into classroom instructional experiences, questions, and assignments.
- *Creative thinking*: Students are provided opportunities to think creatively so that they can develop skills that support original, innovative thinking, elaboration of ideas, flexibility of thought, and problem posing and solving.
- *Problem solving*: Students are engaged in real-world problem solving embedded in scientific processes in sample learning tasks.
- *Technology literacy*: Students use technology in multiple forms and formats as a tool in solving problems and to create generative products.
- *Information media literacy*: Students use multimedia to express ideas, research results, explore real-world problems, and evaluate information presented in media (graphs and diagrams) for scientific accuracy.
- *Social skills*: Students work in small groups and develop the tools of collaboration, communication, and working effectively with others on a common set of tasks.

Relationships Among the NGSS and Other Standards and Skills

To visually demonstrate the relationship between the NGSS and other standards and skills, student practices were examined. Figure 2 highlights some of the relationships between the NAGC Programming Standards, the NGSS (science and engineering practices), and the CCSS in English language arts (student portraits) and mathematics. Practices and portraits were grouped to illustrate student-centered expectations. The midpoint of the graphic demonstrates the relationship across student-centered expectations and/or similar tenets among the four sets of standards. Furthermore, standard–specific student expectations that do not overlap across the four standards are listed in separate boxes. Please note that the graphic does not account for overlapping that may occur among two or three standards (e.g., the use of mathematical and computational thinking in both mathematics and science).

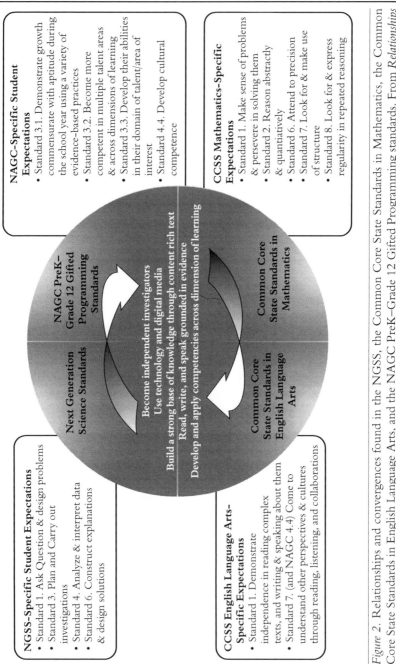

NAGC-Specific Student Expectations
- Standard 3.1. Demonstrate growth commensurate with aptitude during the school year using a variety of evidence-based practices
- Standard 3.2. Become more competent in multiple talent areas & across dimensions of learning
- Standard 3.3. Develop their abilities in their domain of talent/area of interest
- Standard 4.4. Develop cultural competence

CCSS Mathematics-Specific Expectations
- Standard 1. Make sense of problems & persevere in solving them
- Standard 2. Reason abstractly & quantitatively
- Standard 6. Attend to precision
- Standard 7. Look for & make use of structure
- Standard 8. Look for & express regularity in repeated reasoning

NAGC PreK–Grade 12 Gifted Programming Standards

Next Generation Science Standards

Common Core State Standards in Mathematics

Become independent investigators
Use technology and digital media
Build a strong base of knowledge through content rich text
Read, write, and speak grounded in evidence
Develop and apply competencies across dimension of learning

Common Core State Standards in English Language Arts

NGSS-Specific Student Expectations
- Standard 1. Ask Question & design problems
- Standard 3. Plan and Carry out investigations
- Standard 4. Analyze & interpret data
- Standard 6. Construct explanations & design solutions

CCSS English Language Arts-Specific Expectations
- Standard 1. Demonstrate independence in reading complex texts, and writing & speaking about them
- Standard 7. (and NAGC 4.4) Come to understand other perspectives & cultures through reading, listening, and collaborations

Figure 2. Relationships and convergences found in the NGSS, the Common Core State Standards in English Language Arts, and the NAGC PreK–Grade 12 Gifted Programming standards. From *Relationships and Convergences Found in Common Core State Standards in Mathematics, Common Core State Standards in ELA/Literacy, and A Framework for K–12 Science Education,* by T. Cheuk, 2012, Arlington, VA: National Science Teachers Association. Copyright 2012 by NSTA. Adapted with permission.

Linking the NGSS to CCSS in Math and English Language Arts

Because standards often can be addressed across subject areas rather than only in one domain, examples of how to link the NGSS to the CCSS in mathematics and English language arts are included. Other areas of learning that can be applied to standards-based tasks illustrate the efficiency and effectiveness that can be achieved through such compression and the differentiation for gifted learners that results. Dimension 2 of the NGSS, crosscutting concepts, links concepts such as patterns, cause and effect, and systems with each standard. Some of these concepts are also found in the CCSS, making it easier to find points of intersection. Furthermore, specific linkages to the CCSS in math and ELA are found at the bottom of the page of each grade-level topic within the NGSS.

There are two ways to remodel content to engage and motivate highly able learners by making cross–disciplinary connections. Although the strategies are related, they are distinct. The first approach is to use cross–disciplinary content. The second is to integrate standards from science, English language arts, mathematics, or other disciplines. The following are a few examples for each strategy.

Using Cross-Disciplinary Content

This strategy capitalizes on an area of interest in one discipline to engage learners in another. Begin with a standard from the NGSS. Then draw in other content areas to give students opportunities to apply the standard. For example:

- *NGSS HS-PS1-i: Construct an explanation to support predictions about the outcome of simple chemical reactions, using the structure of atoms, trends in the periodic table, and knowledge of the patterns of chemical properties.* The idea in this standard is to identify patterns of chemical properties to construct an explanation to support predictions about the result of simple chemical reactions. Extend this idea beyond science to motivate learners. Ask students to identify and explain patterns in mathematics, in architecture, or in music, as well. Use science to describe and generalize the patterns observed.

- *NGSS 1-ESS1-a. Use observations to describe patterns of objects in the sky that are cyclic and can be predicted.* In this standard, students are going to look for patterns that are cycles. Students might begin studying cycles in other subjects such as economics, music, history, and mathematics. They can then transfer their understanding to science and the sky. Upper grades could look at information about satellites and global positioning systems.

Integrating Standards

This strategy combines standards from two or more disciplines to add complexity. For example:

- *Using NGSS 2-PS1-d: Identify arguments that are supported by evidence that some changes caused by heating or cooling can be reversed and some cannot; Mathematics Standard MP.3: Construct viable arguments and critique the reasoning of others; and English Language Arts Standard W.2.8: Describe how reasons support specific points the author makes in a text.*

Ask students to select one of the following situations: a change caused by heating can be reversed; a change caused by heating cannot be reversed; a change caused by cooling can be reversed; a change caused by cooling cannot be reversed. Students will then develop their argument, using reasons and examples to support their specific points. Students can share their reasoning in small groups and offer critiques of each other's reasoning. Another option would be to have students use a highlighter to identify the reasons they gave to support their arguments.

- *Using NGSS MS-LS1-h: Analyze and interpret provided data to generate evidence supporting the explanation that plants may continue to grow throughout their life through the production of new plant matter via photosynthesis; Mathematics Standard 5.OA: Analyze patterns and relationships and Mathematics Standard 6.EE: Represent and analyze quantitative relationships between dependent and independent variables; and English Language Arts Standard WHST.6-8.9: Write arguments to support claims with clear reasons and relevant evidence.* In responding to the task presented in the science standard, students will need to analyze patterns and relationships. Complexity can be added by using data with dependent and independent variables. Students will need to include clear reasoning and relevant evidence as they construct their arguments to support their explanations.

Cross-disciplinary and integrated approaches are inherent in many research projects that students undertake in science. The writing demonstrates the capacity to build argument, and the construction of mathematical models and analysis of data illustrate the capacity to interpret and transform ideas from graphic representations to verbal ones. By doing so, science, English language arts, and mathematics standards are addressed.

Finding and Developing Talent With NGSS and Gifted Education Strategies

In his seminal work on students who were gifted in science, Brandwein (1988) indicated that creativity and process play essential roles if one wishes to identify students who are gifted and talented in science. Gardner (1995) and Fliegler (1961), along with Brandwein, suggested that science talent may not readily be found by using standard creativity tests and traditional IQ tests because personality factors, competency in science, and a student's previous opportunities to practice the skills of a scientist are not reflected in the scores on these tests. Thus, a better way to find science talent is to watch students working like a practicing professional in the field, identifying a problem and designing an experiment to test the hypothesis. The science and engineering practices will facilitate the opportunities for students to do exactly that. These practices support students in becoming creative producers.

In studying Westinghouse finalists and members of the National Academy of Science, Feist (2006) found that members of both groups wanted at an early age to be scientists. According to Feist, his investigation served to "confirm the importance of early recognition of science talent if creative potential is to become actual creative achievement in adulthood" (p. 32).

To find science talent, teachers will need to observe students engaged in challenging, hands-on, inquiry-based activities such as those that can be designed using all elements of the NGSS: disciplinary core ideas, cross-cutting concepts, science and engineering practices, and links to the CCSS in math and ELA, differentiated for gifted and advanced learners. One example is Project STEM Starters, a Jacob K. Javits Act project that documented the effects of the combination of intensive teacher professional development and the use of inquiry-based science instruction in the elementary classroom, including the benefits of using rigorous science curricula with typical and high-ability students (Cotabish, Dailey, Robinson, & Hughes, 2013). The results of the study revealed a statistically significant gain in science process skills, science concepts, and science content knowledge by students in the experimental group when compared with students in the comparison group.

To create the science innovators of tomorrow, educators need to help students develop passion, perseverance, and creativity in the face of difficult problems and not just scientific competence in knowing facts and problem solving. Higher expectations are needed that include scientific creativity, in which students are encouraged to create their own methods for making sense of and solving problems and raising new questions that are suggested during the solution of the original problem. The science and engineering practices of the NGSS highlight this need.

When students with potential in science participate in accelerated classes that are taught by experienced teachers who are aware of their needs, they are more likely to take rigorous college courses, complete advanced degrees, and feel academically challenged and socially accepted (Colangelo, Assouline, & Gross, 2004; Gross, 2006). Teachers and administrators must be aware of the challenges that gifted students may face when accelerating, particularly if they skip an entire academic year. By using formative assessment and other strategies to identify any gaps in knowledge, teachers can help gifted students to succeed (Chapman, 2009; Siegle & McCoach, 2002).

An instructional option that helps provide creativity and challenge is problem-based learning (PBL). PBL has its roots in the medical field, used to provide medical students with simulations focused on situations that typically arise in one's practice, at the hospital, or in surgery (Gallagher, Sher, Stepien, & Workman, 1995). These researchers adapted it for use in science classes in elementary and high school settings. In addition to integrating PBL and science, the components of all problem-based episodes include

> initiating learning with an ill-structured problem, using the problem to structure the learning agenda, and teacher as metacognitive coach, with important goals of a reformed science curriculum such as learning based on concepts of significance, student-designed experiments, and development of scientific reasoning skills. (p. 137)

Other available options that provide academic challenge are mentorships, dual enrollment, internships, early entrance to college, independent study, and summer programs (Callahan & Kyburg, 2005; Olszewski-Kubilius, 2010; VanTassel-Baska, 2007). There have been some extracurricular programs that show promise, such as museum science programs (Melber, 2003) and afterschool science enrichment programs for girls (Wood, 2002). Results from both programs indicate that students prefer inquiry-based science activities, exactly the kind of activity that is stressed in the NGSS.

The NGSS are designed to provide challenging, inquiry-based science learning experiences. By giving students opportunities to engage in interactive activities that require them to work like professionals in the field, teachers have daily occasions to "kid watch" and observe students who may be demonstrating gifted behaviors in science.

Developing Innovative and Creative Scientists

In the STEM areas, all students, including high-ability students, should be afforded the opportunity to develop their talent. To spur innovation in science, teachers should include an open-ended inquiry approach to teaching and learning, utilize higher order questioning, and provide accelerative learning opportunities to facilitate and advance learning in science. To aid in the development of passionate, innovative, and creative scientists, teachers might use a heuristic such as the one represented in Figure 3.

Using this heuristic, students may start at any point on the diagram and proceed in any order. One possible order might be:

1. Relate the problem to other problems that you have solved. How is this similar to other scientific ideas that you have seen? How is it different?
2. Investigate the problem. Think deeply and ask questions.
3. Evaluate your findings. Did you answer the question? Does the answer make sense?
4. Communicate your results. How can you best let others know what you have discovered?
5. Create new questions to explore. What else would you

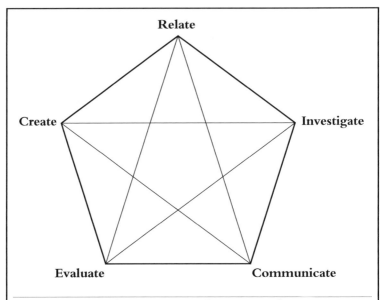

Figure 3. Heuristic for innovative and creative mathematicians. From *Extending the Challenge in Mathematics: Developing Mathematical Promise in K–8 Students* (p. 15), by L. J. Sheffield, 2003, Thousand Oaks, CA: Corwin Press. Copyright 2003 by Corwin Press. Reprinted with permission.

like to find out about this topic? Start a new investigation.

To assist students in their creation of new scientific insights, some suggested questions for creative scientific investigations are (Sheffield, 2006):

- *Who?* Who has another solution? Who has another method? Who agrees or disagrees?
- *What or what if?* What patterns do I see in this data? What generalizations might I make from the patterns? What proof do I have? What are the chances? What is the best answer, best method of solution, best strategy to begin with? What if I change one or more parts of the problem? What new problems might I create?
- *When?* When does this work? When does this not work?

- *Where?* Where did that come from? Where should I start? Where might I go next? Where might I find additional information?
- *Why or why not?* Why does that work? If it does not work, why does it not work?
- *How?* How is this like other scientific problems or patterns that I have seen? How does it differ? How does this relate to real-life situations or models? How many solutions are possible? How many ways might I use it to represent, simulate, model, or visualize these ideas? How many ways might I sort, organize, and present this information?

Depth and Complexity

Even our best science students are not often encouraged to be creative. Educators need to support them as they move from questions with one right answer to those that require reasoning and justification and to problems and explorations that have several solutions or related problems that will deepen and extend the concepts being learned. Educators need to remember that the real learning frequently begins after the original problem has been solved.

If educators wish for students to develop deeper understanding of concepts and become creative investigative scientists, they should use criteria for assessment that encourage depth and complexity, such as:

- *Depth of understanding:* the extent to which core concepts are understood, explored, and developed;
- *Fluency:* the number of different correct answers, methods of solution, or new questions formulated;
- *Flexibility:* the number of different categories of answers, methods, or questions;
- *Originality:* solutions, methods, or questions that are unique and show insight;

- *Elaboration or elegance:* clarity and quality of expression of thinking, including charts, graphs, drawings, models, and words;
- *Generalizations:* patterns that are noted, hypothesized, and verified for larger categories; and
- *Extensions:* related questions that are asked and explored, especially those involving why and what if.

Instructional Pace

The instructional pace is also a critical consideration in the education of gifted students in science. Advanced learners may demonstrate rapid or early mastery of some of the NGSS standards, especially those involving skill at problem solving and mastery of content, requiring accelerative opportunities at key stages of development. Appropriate pacing for these students, including in accelerated courses, means that students have the time and opportunity to delve deeply and creatively into topics, projects and problems, models, and theories of interest. Previous research demonstrates that curriculum acceleration or accelerative learning is one of the most effective interventions for gifted students (Colangelo et al., 2004; Swiatek & Benbow, 1992). It's important, therefore, that advanced learners receive their instruction from well-prepared teachers who are knowledgeable in science and familiar with strategies to use with advanced learners.

Stimulating Scientific Thinking

Teachers of the gifted should be mindful of the importance of providing inquiry and investigative skills and strategies to stimulate scientific reasoning and work with a wide range of scientific topics grounded in biology, chemistry, and physics and mathematical topics such as number theory, geometry, and discrete mathematics. Early exposure to topics such as probability, statistics, and logic also are viable approaches to be used to support applied and cross-curricular skills, including conducting meaningful research in science and engineering. Extracurricular opportunities such as science clubs, competitions, mentors, and online experiences should also be readily available without additional cost for the students.

In encouraging these high levels of creativity and giftedness (Chapin, O'Connor, & Anderson, 2009), teachers should realize that the role of the student is to:

- think, reason, make sense, and go deeper;
- talk to a partner and generate new ideas;
- repeat and rephrase what others have said and explain why he or she agrees or disagrees;
- make generalizations and justify conclusions;
- add on new ideas, new methods of solution, new questions, and original problems and related solutions;
- record solutions, reasoning, and questions;
- pose new scientific questions of interest to investigate; and
- create innovative scientific problems and solutions.

The role of the teacher is to:

- ask questions that encourage scientific creativity, reasoning, and sense making;
- elicit, engage, and challenge each student's thinking;
- listen carefully to students' ideas;
- ask students to clarify, justify, connect, and extend their ideas;
- assist students in attaching mathematical notation and scientific language to their ideas;
- reflect on student understanding, differentiate instruction, and encourage participation; and
- guide students to resources, including online, in print, and in person such as mentors, apprenticeships, competitions, clubs, and other extracurricular opportunities.

Early exposure to scientific thinking and processes can stimulate innovation (National Science Board, 2010). Providing a challenging learning environment that includes advanced questioning, depth and complexity, and adjustments for instructional pace can facilitate a bridge between scientific knowledge, skills, and processes.

Four Major Strategies for Gifted Education

There are four major strategies that may be employed to accomplish the task for gifted education. Individually, each strategy is an important component to meet the needs of high-ability science learners. Ideally, it is important to view them as a coherent system of strategies rather than autonomous tasks.

Provide pathways with appropriate pacing of the NGSS for gifted learners. Some of the NGSS address higher level skills and concepts that should receive focus throughout the years of schooling, such as a major emphasis on reasoning and sense making. However, there are also discrete skills that may be clustered across grade levels and compressed around higher level skills and concepts for more efficient mastery by gifted students. Teachers might use preassessments in determining which students require more accelerated pacing. For example, within the DCI of matter and its interactions, some students in second grade might test objects made from different materials to determine if a proposed object functions as intended (e.g., strength, flexibility, hardness, texture) while others make observations and measurements to identify given materials based on their properties (Grade 5 PSI-C).

Provide examples of differentiated task demands to address specific standards. Standards in science lend themselves to differentiated interpretation through demonstrating what a typical learner on grade level might be able to do at a given stage of development versus what a gifted learner might be able to do. The differentiated examples should show greater complexity and creativity, using a more advanced curriculum base. In science, although typical learners might investigate models and theories using a variety of strategies, gifted learners might pose and solve new, related models and theories of their own at an earlier stage of development. Other degrees of differentiation may take place by adding complexity to the task and using enrichment techniques, such as using scientific inquiry and modeling to solve community problems that address student needs and community demographics.

Create interdisciplinary product demands to elevate learning for gifted students and to efficiently address multiple standards at once. Because many of the science and CCSS English language arts and mathematics standards can be grouped together in application, much of the project work that gifted educators might already use could be revised to connect to the new NGSS and CCSS in mathematics and show how multiple standards could be addressed across content areas. For example, science-based research projects could be designed that address the research standard in English language arts and the data representation standard in mathematics by (a) delineating a product demand for research on an issue, (b) asking researchable questions that require quantitative approaches, (c) using multiple sources to answer them, (d) collecting data, (e) interpreting data and describing the related variables, and (f) representing findings in tables, graphs, and other visual displays that are explained in text and presented to an audience with implications for a plan of action. Such a project might be possible for the gifted learner at an earlier grade than for a typical learner.

Use gifted and talented curriculum to develop scientific literacy. The CCSS literacy standards supplement and support the need for reading, writing, speaking, listening, and language as it pertains to science. The field of gifted education has existing gifted education curriculum guides to support integrated science literacy. For example, the *Blueprints for Biography* (Robinson, 2009–2011) is a series of teacher curriculum guides with high-level discussion questions, creative and critical thinking activities, a persuasive writing component, and rich primary resources. Each concludes with a classic experiment for students to carry out. STEM *Blueprints* focus on eminent scientists and inventors for whom exemplary children's biographies exist in trade book form.

U-STARS Plus Science and Literature Connections (Coleman & Shah-Coltrane, 2010) provides an engaging way to explore scientific ideas within literacy instruction time using 32 popular children's books. Most of the selected books are readily available and many of the books have been translated into Spanish. *Science and Literature Connections* is organized around Bloom's taxonomy to support a range of thinking levels and to scaffold learning. By using these materials, a teacher can create a higher level thinking environment around literature connected with science that motivates reluctant readers. The science concepts are based on the National Science Education Standards and align nicely with the NGSS. *Science and Literature Connections* was designed for grades K–3; however, many of the "connections" may be adapted for grades 4–5.

Other science curricula for high-ability learners have integrated literacy connections. For example, the William and Mary science curriculum units, including problem-based science units, and Project Clarion units have taken an integrated approach to address science literacy while addressing scientific concepts and processes. All of the William and Mary science units reinforce reading, writing, speaking, listening, and language as it pertains to science.

Sample Learning Experiences for Advanced and Gifted Students in Science

The following pages offer examples of activities to support the implementation of the NGSS. The sample activities were designed to give exemplars in a variety of areas including motion and stability (forces and interactions), Earth's systems (weather and climate), and life sciences (botany). Moreover, the exemplars include sections that denote both Crosscutting Concepts and Science and Engineering Practices (see section titled *Three Dimensions of the Next Generation Science Standards* on p. xvii for discussion).

Sample activities are provided for primary, intermediate, middle, and high school standards. Each activity begins with a selected task, gives a variety of questions for both typical and advanced learners, and describes suggestions for implementation that include ideas for different types of formative and summative assessment. Note that sometimes the initial problem is the same for both typical and advanced learners, using questions and formative assessments to differentiate and develop scientific creativity and giftedness.

Formative assessment in these activities includes the use of pretests, differentiation of tasks, and questions to assess during the problem-solving process, observation and analysis of student work, and authentic cross-disciplinary tasks and research.

There are two additional elements embedded within the NGSS associated with the performance expectations that are meant to render additional support and clarity:

- *Assessment boundary statements* are included with individual performance expectations where appropriate to provide further guidance or to specify the scope of the expectation at a particular grade level.
- *Clarification statements* are designed to supply examples or additional clarification to the performance expectations.

Assessment boundary and clarification statements should not limit teaching and learning. They are meant to provide guidance as they plan instruction. For more about assessment boundary and clarification statements, see discussion on page 53.

Sample Learning Experiences K–8

Grade K Motion and Stability: Forces and Interactions	Teacher Information: Typical learners should have the background knowledge in using rulers and meter sticks before participating in this instructional experience. Advanced learners will already have a good understanding of measurement (meters, centimeters) and will be ready to move to higher order concepts, such as velocity. Teachers will need floor space for each group to complete this activity. Materials: This lesson requires the following materials: ball, masking tape, ruler, meter stick, and a book for each group.	
	Typical Learners	Advanced Learners
	Essential Question: How do you determine whether an object is still or moving?	

Standard(s):
  K-PS2-1. Plan and conduct an investigation to compare the effects of different strengths or different directions of pushes and pulls on the motion of an object. *Clarification Statement*: Examples of pushes or pulls could include a string attached to an object being pulled, a person pushing an object, a person stopping a rolling ball, and two objects colliding and pushing on each other. *Assessment Boundary*: Assessment is limited to different relative strengths or different directions, but not both at the same time. Assessment does not
continued
	Directions: Begin with a preassessment using brainstorming. Ask students, "How do we know when an object is still or moving?" After listening to student answers, have students measure distances of 3 cm, 22 cm, and 1 meter to check for understanding of how to measure distances using centimeters and meters. Reteach those who have forgotten how to measure with standard measures.
	  Divide students into small groups (two to four). Give each group a ball, masking tape, rulers, and meter sticks. Place a piece of masking tape on the floor. Place a tennis ball on the tape. Have students write a response to the following questions:
	1. Is the tennis ball still or moving?
	2. How do you know?
	continued
		Directions: In addition to demonstrating the concepts expected of typical learners, advanced learners will be introduced to the concept of velocity. Explain that *velocity* tells how fast an object is moving and in which direction it is moving.
		  Advanced learners may find the direction that an object moves (in this case, a ball). The teacher will need to prepare by doing the following:
		1. Determine where the north wall of the room is located.
		2. Make a tag board card with the word "north" written on it.
		3. Repeat this procedure for each of the other three directions.
		continued

Grade K: Motion and Stability, *continued*

include noncontact pushes or pulls such as those produced by magnets.

K-PS2-2. Analyze data to determine if a design solution works as intended to change the speed or direction of an object with a push or a pull. *Clarification Statement:* Examples of problems requiring a solution could include having a marble or other object move a certain distance, follow a particular path, and knock down other objects. Examples of solutions could include tools such as a ramp to increase the speed of the object and a structure that would cause an object such as a marble or ball to turn. *Assessment Boundary:* Assessment does not include friction as a mechanism for change in speed.

Next, ask students to give the tennis ball a gentle push. Have students write a response to the following questions:

1. Is the tennis ball still or moving after you pushed it?
2. How do you know?

Now, place a piece of tape at the spot where the tennis ball stops. Use a ruler or meter stick to measure the distance between the two pieces of tape (emphasizing the utilization of correct units).

A handout or table could be given to each group for recording data and could include the following:

1. Distance between the pieces of tape
2. Explain how to find out if an object is in motion.

Ask students to repeat the activity, this time pushing the ball with greater strength. Have students write a response to the following questions:

1. What is the distance between the pieces of tape?
2. Explain what occurred to the ball when you applied greater force?

Next, explain to students that they are going to measure a different motion. Ask students to place a

continued

Give each group of two students a ball, masking tape, ruler, and stopwatch. One student will be responsible for keeping time with the stopwatch while the other student will be responsible for pushing the tennis ball. Explain that the stopwatch will be utilized to time the tennis ball until it comes to a rest.

Students will measure the distance between the two pieces of tape and record their answers. They will need to be reminded that they are to use the correct units of measurement. A handout or table could be given to each group for recording data and could include the following:

1. Distance between the pieces of tape _____
2. Time to travel this distance _____
3. In what direction did the tennis ball move (north, south, east, west)? _____

Students will repeat the steps, but switch places with their partner.

Once the activities are completed, the teacher should meet with students in small groups to discuss their results.

Advanced learners will answer the following questions:

continued

Grade K: Motion and Stability, *continued*

piece of masking tape on the floor and to place a book on the tape to serve as a barrier.

Ask students the following questions:
1. Is the book still or moving?
2. How do you know?

Next, students are to roll the ball toward the book. Ask students to respond to the following questions:
1. What happened to the ball once it hit the book?
2. What distance did the ball travel before hitting the book?

Last, tell students to slowly lift the book off the floor. Ask students the following questions:
1. Is the book still or moving while you are lifting it?
2. How do you know?

Students should ask their partner to measure from the floor to the book's elevated height. They should record their answer in the correct units.

Ask students to discuss their answers with another group and determine the similarities and differences in their answers.

Once these activities are completed, meet with the students in small groups to discuss their results.

Conclude the lesson by revisiting the question they were asked to consider in the introduction: How

continued

1. In what direction did the tennis ball move (north, south, east, west, toward the window, toward the chair)?
2. What was the distance between the pieces of tape?
3. How long did it take to travel this distance?

For an additional challenge, ask students to repeat the activity using various rolling objects (with different masses). At the conclusion of the activity, ask students the following questions:
1. How did the motion of the first object (ball), differ from the second (or third, etc.) object?
2. How did the distance differ?
3. How did the time differ?
4. How did the direction differ?
5. What do you think contributed to the differences?

Conclude the lesson by revisiting the question they were asked to consider in the introduction: How can we explain velocity? How is it different from motion? (Students should conclude that an object is in motion when its distance from another object is changing. Velocity tells how fast an object is moving and in which direction it is moving.)

For additional challenge, advanced students could calculate velocity because they have all of the variables.

Grade K: Motion and Stability, *continued*	
	can we tell whether an object is still or in motion? (Students should conclude that an object is in motion when its distance from another object is changing).
Implementation	The teacher convenes a whole-class meeting. The teacher explains to the students that they are going to talk about motion in this lesson. The teacher asks students to describe and brainstorm "motion." The brainstorming session can be a quick preassessment to see who understands the concept of motion. The teacher asks students to consider the following question: How do we know when an object is still or in motion? Furthermore, this activity will require typical students to measure distances in meters and centimeters, and advanced learners will build on measurement skills by considering the effects of time and direction (velocity). After whole-group instruction, typical and advanced students will work in small groups or groups of two. The teacher then meets with the advanced learners to discuss their answers to the questions. To further explain velocity, the teacher could use real-life scenarios or examples. For example, the teacher could pose the following questions: • How fast does your mom drive? • What is the velocity of your fastball? Posing such questions could encourage students to determine the velocity variables.
Crosscutting Concepts	**Cause and Effect:** Simple tests can be designed to gather evidence to support or refute student ideas about causes.
Science and Engineering Practices	**Asking Questions and Defining Problems:** Formulate questions that can be investigated and predict reasonable outcomes based on patterns such as cause and effect relationships. **Planning and Carrying Out Investigations:** Design and conduct investigations collaboratively, using fair tests in which variables are controlled and the number of trials considered. Make observations and/or measurements, collect appropriate data, and identify patterns that provide evidence for an explanation of a phenomenon or test a design solution.

Note: Lesson implementation is adapted from *May the Force Be With You: Still or Moving,* by C. Adams, 2013. Unpublished lesson for Project Conn-cept. Adapted with permission.

Grade 3 Motion and Stability: Forces and Interactions	**Teacher Information:** This activity will require typical students to predict the effects of balanced and unbalanced forces on an object while manipulating one variable at a time. Advanced learners will carry out investigations that require the measurement of force while manipulating up to two variables at a time. **Materials:** Spring scales (one per group), one meter piece of string per group, meter stick (one per group), several small toys per group (car, ping pong ball, block. etc.)

Typical Learners	**Advanced Learners**

Essential Question: How does a force make an object stop, move, or change direction?

Standard(s): **3-PS2-1. Plan and conduct an investigation to provide evidence of the effects of balanced and unbalanced forces on the motion of an object.** *Clarification Statement:* Examples could include that an unbalanced force on one side of a ball can make it start moving and balanced forces pushing on a box from both sides will not produce any motion at all. *Assessment Boundary:* Assessment is limited to one variable at a time: number, size, or direction of forces. Assessment does not include quantitative force size, only qualitative and relative. Assessment is limited to gravity being addressed as a force that pulls objects down. **3-PS2-2. Make observations and/ or measurements of an object's** *continued*	**Directions:** This activity assumes that the teacher has introduced Newton's Second and Third Laws of Motion. To facilitate this activity, the teacher would divide students into groups of two to four. Give each group five objects. Have students make each one move to understand the concept that when something moves, a force makes it move. Students may use a piece of string to tie around objects to create "pull" movement. Students will construct a table and place an "X" in the appropriate column to indicate how they made each object move. Example: 	Object	Force (How we made it move; push and pull)	
	Push	**Pull**
			  continued	**Directions:** Advanced learners will learn how to measure a force by using a spring scale and the same objects that typical learners used. They will measure the force that is used to move an object in newtons (N). Students will: (1) choose an object, (2) set the spring scale to zero, (3) hook the object on the scale, (4) observe the scale to see if the bar has moved, noting the measurement in newtons, (5) create a chart to record how many newtons of force were needed to move each object, (6) repeat the same steps with each of the other objects. After completing the instructional experience, have students answer the following questions in their science journal: 1. Which object required the most force to move? 2. Which object required the least force to move? 3. How can you make a real car move by pushing or pulling it? Next, students will predict the effect of forces on an object in terms of balanced forces that do not change motion and unbalanced forces that change *continued*

Grade 3: Motion and Stability, *continued*

motion to provide evidence that a pattern can be used to predict future motion. *Clarification Statement:* Examples of motion with a predictable pattern could include a child swinging in a swing, a ball rolling back and forth in a bowl, and two children on a seesaw. *Assessment Boundary:* Assessment does not include technical terms such as period and frequency.	After completing the instructional experience, ask students to push on one side of an object with the same amount of force as their partner on the opposite side and answer the following questions in their science journal: 1. What happened? 2. Which object was the easiest to push or pull? Explain. 3. Which object was the hardest to pull? Explain. 4. Why didn't the object move when you and your partner pushed with equal forces? Did your object change direction? If so, why? After answering the questions, ask students to draw a picture to show what happened when both students pushed with equal force on the same object. Next, students will predict the effect of forces on an object in terms of balanced forces that do not change motion and unbalanced forces that change motion. For this part of the activity, students will be given a different set of objects (up to three per group). They will draw a picture to show what they predict what will happen when a force is applied either by pushing or pulling, and what they expect to happen when both students would push with equal force on the same object. Ask students to answer the following questions: 1. Which object did you predict to be the easiest to push or pull? Explain. *continued*	motion. For this part of the activity, students will predict the outcome of the trials using the same objects but will consider the manipulation of two variables. Students will draw their prediction, noting the number, size, or direction of forces when manipulating two variables. Ask students to answer the following questions: 1. How did manipulating two variables change your outcome? 2. What was surprising about your outcome? 3. How could you change the motion of other objects? 4. Predict a future motion of a selected object using the concepts of size, force, and direction. For additional challenge, students can test their prediction by repeating the activity while manipulating two variables. Conclude the activity by asking students to consider the following scenario: A student and one partner agreed to play tug-of-war on the playground. Rules were in place that prevented each from letting go of the rope. How could you predict who would win? What variables would you consider? How can changing the variables affect the outcome? Devise an experiment to test your prediction.

Grade 3: Motion and Stability, *continued*	
	2. Which object did you predict to be the hardest to pull? Explain. 3. What did you predict would happen to the object when you and your partner pushed with equal forces? Explain. 4. Did you predict that any of the objects would change direction when a force was applied? Why or why not? Conclude the activity by asking students to consider the following scenario: A student and one partner agreed to play tug-of-war on the playground. Rules were in place that prevented each from letting go of the rope. How could you predict who would win? What variables would you consider?
Implementation	The teacher convenes a whole-class meeting. The teacher explains to the students that they are going to talk about force in this lesson. The teacher asks students to describe and brainstorm "force." The brainstorming session can be a quick preassessment to see who understands the concept of force. The teacher asks students to consider the following question: How do we know which objects are easiest to push or pull? What happens when two objects collide with equal force? After whole-group instruction, typical and advanced students will work in small groups or groups of two to four. Use an observation checklist to keep track of student progress. Give students increasingly difficult challenges as they work individually or with a partner who is at a similar level. Encourage advanced learners to manipulate two variables at a time as they participate in the learning experience.
Crosscutting Concepts	**Cause and Effect:** Cause and effect relationships are routinely identified, tested, and used to explain change.

Grade 3: Motion and Stability, continued	
Science and Engineering Practices	**Asking Questions and Defining Problems:** Formulate questions that can be investigated and predict reasonable outcomes based on patterns such as cause and effect relationships. **Planning and Carrying Out Investigations:** Design and conduct investigations collaboratively, using fair tests in which variables are controlled and the number of trials considered. Make observations and/or measurements, collect appropriate data, and identify patterns that provide evidence for an explanation of a phenomenon or test a design solution. **Scientific Investigations Using a Variety of Methods:** Science investigations use a variety of tools and techniques. There is not one scientific method.

Note: Lesson implementation is adapted from *May the Force Be With You: Still or Moving*, by C. Adams, 2013. Unpublished lesson for Project Conn–cept. Adapted with permission.

Middle School
Motion and Stability:
Forces and Interactions

Teacher Information: Typical learners will attempt to model variable factors that may affect the acceleration of an object by using a dynamics cart. Advanced learners will predict what will affect acceleration, construct a diagram with calculations, and carry out their own trials.

Materials: Dynamics cart, laboratory masses or bricks, timing device, string, and spring scales. Forces can be measured with either force sensors or spring scales. Accelerations can be determined by using meter sticks and stopwatches, ticker timers, or motion detectors with computer-based laboratory tools or calculator-based laboratory tools.

Essential Questions: What factors do you think might affect the acceleration of an object? What relationships exist between force and acceleration? Mass and acceleration?

Typical Learners	Advanced Learners
Directions: Explain to students that objects change their motion only when a net force is applied. Laws of motion are used to calculate precisely the effects of forces on the motion of objects. (The magnitude of the change in motion can be calculated using the relationship $F = ma$, which is independent of the nature of the force.) Whenever one object exerts a force on another, a force equal in magnitude and opposite in direction is exerted on the first object. Tell students they will play the role of researchers. They will hypothesize what variables will affect acceleration of an object and design an experiment to show the relationship. In this activity, students will attempt to model the factors that may affect the acceleration of an object by using a dynamics cart. Dynamics carts generally have minimal friction, so friction can be ignored (friction would not have to be ignored with advanced students). For each variable that is identified to have *continued*	**Directions:** Advanced learners will consider a cart on a horizontal surface. The cart is propelled by a falling mass. Students will construct a free-body diagram for both the falling mass and the accelerating cart. Students will construct a diagram with equations to calculate the acceleration of the cart and the mass. Moreover, students will predict factors of acceleration and the relationship between force and acceleration. 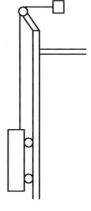 Students will need to keep in mind that the falling mass and the cart are connected, which means both objects have the same acceleration. *continued*

Standard(s):
MS-PS2-2. Plan an investigation to provide evidence that the change in an object's motion depends on the sum of the forces on the object and the mass of the object. *Clarification Statement:* Emphasis is on balanced (Newton's First Law) and unbalanced forces in a system, qualitative comparisons of forces, mass and changes in motion (Newton's Second Law), frame of reference, and specification of units. *Assessment Boundary:* Assessment is limited to forces and changes in motion in one-dimension in an inertial reference frame and to change in one variable at a time. Assessment does not include the use of trigonometry.

Middle School: Motion and Stability, *continued*

an effect on acceleration, students will conduct an experiment to determine whether that variable does affect the acceleration. Students should be given a chance to organize their own experiments in groups of four. If students need some help, the teacher might suggest a way to measure a constant force over a distance with a dynamics cart and timer. Attaching a string to the cart and hanging a mass attached to the string over the edge of a table, as shown below, could do this. Note that the weight of the hanging mass is not the force exerted on the car. The tension in the string is the force that accelerates the cart. (Note: The tension is equal to the weight of the hanging mass minus the mass of the system times its acceleration—teachers may want to share this with advanced learners.) Force sensors and spring scales also can be used to measure the force exerted on the cart.

Cart Mass (m_2)

F_T ⟶

Direction of Motion (+)

F_{weight}

Floor

continued

Students will test their predictions by attempting to model the factors of acceleration displayed in their diagram and calculate the acceleration of the cart and the mass. Furthermore, students will test the relationship between force and acceleration.

Ask students, "Does the predicted acceleration agree with the experimental value?" Tell students to demonstrate their answer by showing all work.

After conducting the trials, students will provide a qualitative assessment of their findings. Students are asked to respond to the following questions:

1. If an object is not accelerating, can you conclude that no forces are acting on it?

2. If we say that one quantity is proportional to another quantity, does this statement also mean they are equal to each other? Explain using mass and weight in your example.

To enhance the concept with advanced learners, the teacher will discuss dependent and independent variables, and reinforce the concept that force and mass are independent variables because they can be changed by manipulating their values. A debriefing of results and their findings should reinforce the understanding that force is directly related to acceleration, and acceleration is inversely related to mass. This relationship can be summarized as: The acceleration of an object is directly proportional to the force on the

continued

Middle School: Motion and Stability, *continued*

Students may devise a method of measuring the acceleration achieved by a given force. The force can be increased. Students then can plot force versus acceleration graphs and mass versus acceleration graphs and evaluate results. They should collect data for at least five different forces in order to obtain a meaningful graph. Students should run three to five trials for each different variable. Students will determine and record the acceleration for each trial in a data table.

Using graph paper or a computer program, students will graph their results and describe the appearance of each graph.

To conclude the activity, students will provide a qualitative assessment of their findings. Students are asked to respond to the following questions:

1. What relationships exist between force and acceleration? Mass and acceleration?
2. How do you know these relationships exist?
3. What are some examples of force and acceleration at work in everyday life?
4. What variables would you need to consider to change the direction of object(s) you referred to as examples in question 3? Is it testable? How?

To sum it up, acceleration increases as the force increases when the mass is constant (direct proportion). Acceleration decreases as the mass increases if the force remains constant (inverse proportion).

object and inversely proportional to the mass of the object.

$$a = F/m$$

Explain that this is a form of Newton's Second Law. The force in this equation is actually the net force acting on an object, which means that you have to add up all of the forces on the object that you are trying to accelerate. This relationship often is solved algebraically for force, and can be written as

$$F_{net} = ma$$

Additional challenge could include introducing frictional and applied force, net force, and terminal velocity.

To conclude the activity, ask students to graph their previous findings, illustrating acceleration versus force. An example graph is included below:

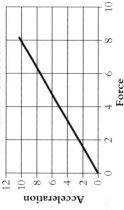

Acceleration Versus Force

Middle School: Motion and Stability, *continued*	
Implementation	The teacher should recognize that controlling all of the variables, sketching graphs, and analyzing them requires rather formal reasoning. In the spirit of an exploratory activity, the teacher should allow all students to determine their own way to find solutions to the general questions posed and to exhibit different exit levels of learning by experimentation. In addition, advanced learners will use predictive measures and test their predictions when carrying out the activity. The teacher will have a chance to increase student understanding of Newton's Laws during postlab discussions.
Science and Engineering Practices	**Asking Questions and Defining Problems:** Design an investigation individually and collaboratively. In the design, identify independent and dependent variables and controls, what tools are needed to do the gathering, how measurements will be recorded, and how much data are needed to support the claim. **Scientific Knowledge Is Based on Empirical Evidence:** Science knowledge is based on logical conceptual connections between evidence and explanations. Science disciplines share common rules of obtaining and evaluating empirical evidence.

Note: Lesson implementation is adapted from PRISMS Plus (CD version) by T. M. Cooney, L. T. Escalada, and R. D. Unruh, 2008, Cedar Falls, IA: University of Northern Iowa Physics Department. Copyright 2008 by UNI Physics Department. Adapted with permission.

High School (Course 1) Motion and Stability: Forces and Interactions	**Teacher information:** Typical learners will investigate the effects of a variable force acting on a constant mass in relation to acceleration and frictional force. Advanced learners should explore multidimensional relationships between mass, acceleration, frictional force, and momentum. The creation of equations to predict outcomes along with the manipulation of variables will add challenge to the activity **Materials:** Low friction carts (or skateboards), three 20 N spring balances, meter stick, and two stopwatches per group.	
	Typical Learners	**Advanced Learners**
	Essential Question: How does the magnitude and direction of the force (applied or frictional) affect the acceleration of an object?	
Standard(s): HS-PS2-1. Analyze data to support the claim that Newton's Second Law of Motion describes the mathematical relationship among the net force on a macroscopic object, its mass, and its acceleration. *Clarification Statement:* Examples of data could include tables or graphs of position or velocity as a function of time for objects subject to a net unbalanced force, such as a falling object, an object rolling down a ramp, or a moving object being pulled by a constant force. *Assessment Boundary:* Assessment is limited to one-dimensional motion and to macroscopic objects moving at nonrelativistic speeds.	**Directions:** Students will work in groups of four to five. Students will select a starting point and mark a point that is 10 meters away in a direction that has an extended coast zone beyond the 10-meter line. The student on the cart must grasp the hook on the spring balance with one hand and a door frame (immovable object) with the other. A student can be used as the immovable object. A second student must grasp the other end of the spring balance and exert a constant 20 N force on the rider. On a signal, the student will start the first timer as the rider releases from the doorframe. The puller must maintain a constant 20-N force throughout the 10-meter measured distance, regardless of the temptation to pull harder to "get going." At the 10-meter line stop the first watch, start the second watch, and have the rider release his or her grasp on the spring balance. *continued*	**Directions:** In addition to demonstrating the concepts expected of typical learners, advanced learners will create an equation that will predict acceleration if mass, accelerating force, and frictional force are all known. Acceleration equals the accelerating force (net force) divided by the mass only if frictional forces are not considered part of the accelerating force. Considering friction, the equation becomes: $$F_{net} = F_{applied} + F_{friction}$$ So $$a = F_{net}/m = (F_{applied} + F_{friction})/m$$ Note that the value for friction is in the opposite direction to the applied force (scale reading and will be negative. F_{net} is the vector sum of all forces. *continued*

High School (Course 1): Motion and Stability, *continued*

Stop the second stopwatch when the cart coasts to a stop. Spotters may be needed at the 10-meter line and along the coast path to keep the rider in an "upright position." Repeat several times until fairly consistent timings and distances are recorded, average these results and have students enter on a data table. (An example data table is included in the Implementation section).

Repeat procedures using the same skater/puller team with 40 N and 60 N forces.

Sample Observations/Calculations (Constant 20 N Force)

1. Mass of student and cart 67 kg
2. Time for acceleration 9.89 s
3. Average velocity = 10m/9.89 s = 1.01 m/s
4. Initial velocity = 0 m/s
5. Final velocity = (2 x average velocity) = 2.02 m/s
6. If average velocity = $(v_1 + v_2)/2$

Acceleration = $\dfrac{v_2 - v_1}{t}$

$\dfrac{2.02ms - 0}{9.89s} = .204 m/s^2$

7. Accelerating force or $F_{net} = ma = (67\ kg)(2.04\ m/s^2) = 136.7\ N$
8. Coasting time = 20.5 s
9. Initial velocity = 2.02 m/s (velocity at 10 m line from "5" on data table)

continued

Ask students the following question: If an average net force of 50 N delivered by a bicyclist produces an acceleration of 1.5 m/s², what acceleration would you predict for the same cyclist on the same bicycle if the cyclist applied a net force of 75 N?

Answer: Because acceleration is directly related or proportional to the net force on the object, one could write the equation as

$$F1/a1 = F2/a2$$

$$(1.5\ m/s^2)/(a_2) = (50\ N)/(75\ N)$$

$$a_2 = (3/2)(1.5\ m/s^2)\ \text{or}\ a_2 = 2.25\ m/s^2$$

After students demonstrate understanding, students will consider how the equation will change with unknown variable(s).

To extend the activity, advanced learners may investigate related concepts. For example, students could design an investigation to support the claim that the total momentum is conserved when there is no net force on the system.

When an object is moving, it has a nonzero momentum. If an object is standing still, then its momentum is zero.

To calculate the momentum, students will multiply the mass times the velocity.

Momentum = mass x velocity or p = mv

continued

High School (Course 1): Motion and Stability, *continued*

	Sample Observations/Calculations (using average velocity)
10. Final velocity = 0 11. Acceleration = $\dfrac{v_2 - v_1}{t}$ $= \dfrac{0 - 2.02m/s}{20.5s} = -0.0985m/s^2$ 12. Friction force = $(67\ kg)(-0.0985\ m/s^2) = -6.60N$ After conducting the trials, students are to provide a qualitative assessment of their findings. Students are asked to respond to the following questions: 1. What is the relationship between frictional force, accelerating force, and the measure force? 2. Does it appear that frictional forces act during the first 10 m? Explain. 3. Lines 6 and 11 from the table may have positive and negative signs. Explain the reasons for these signs. 4. Lines 7 and 12 may have positive and negative signs. Explain the reasons for these signs. At the conclusion of the activity, ask students how motion will change if the force is increased to 80 N and the cart is allowed to coast to a stop. Students should recognize that friction is a force that opposes motion and is considered a negative number *continued*	$p = (67.0\ kg)(1.01\ m/s)$ $p = 67.67$ kg-m/s Therefore, the momentum of the object is calculated to be 67.67 kg-m/s (pronounced "kilogram meter per second"). Momentum is a quantity that has a magnitude, or size, and a direction. The term "vector" can be introduced (if not previously taught) or reinforced when asking students to calculate momentum. Students can sketch momentum of a trial (with the understanding that there is an assumption of moving along a straight line). For additional challenge, advanced learners may want to calculate the direction (positive, negative) in two and three dimensions.

High School (Course 1): Motion and Stability, *continued*

	if the velocity direction is positive. Station spotters should be located at the 10-meter line to reduce the possibilities of falls. Insist that the students maintain a constant force on the spring balances and resist temptations to pull harder at the starting line or give an extra push at the 10-meter line. To extend the activity, students would observe types of motion outside of class, and then return with descriptions of the events in terms of forces, velocities, changes in velocity, acceleration, and mass. Some examples might be collisions of cars at intersections, a football player getting pushed out of bounds while running down field, and the motions of a baseball in flight toward center field. The teacher may want to suggest that students also look at cases when the force is not along the same line with the velocity.
Implementation	The data collection takes one class period. Another class period is needed for discussion, qualitative assessments, and quantitative calculations. Students are asked to generate their own data table or the following example may be used: *continued*

High School (Course 1): Motion and Stability, *continued*

	20 N Trial	40 N Trial	60 N Trial
1. Mass of student and cart			
2. Time for acceleration			
3. Average velocity during acceleration			
4. Initial velocity			
5. Final velocity			
6. Acceleration			
7. Accelerating force (F_{net})			
Applies only to the coasting segment of each trial			
8. Coasting time			
9. Initial velocity (from above)			
10. Final velocity (stopped)			
11. Acceleration			
12. Frictional force			

Crosscutting Concepts	**Systems and System Models:** Models can be used to represent systems and their interactions—such as inputs, processes, and outputs—and energy, matter, and information flows within systems. Models are limited in that they only represent certain aspects of the system under study.
Science and Engineering Practices	**Analyzing and Interpreting Data:** Use tools, technologies, and/or models (e.g., computational, mathematical) to generate and analyze data in order to make valid and reliable scientific claims or determine an optimal design solution.

Note: Lesson implementation is adapted from PRISMS Plus (CD version) by T. M. Cooney, L. T. Escalada, and R. D. Unruh, 2008, Cedar Falls, IA: University of Northern Iowa Physics Department. Copyright 2008 by UNI Physics Department. Adapted with permission.

Grade K Earth's Systems: Weather and Climate	**Teacher Information:** Typical learners should have background knowledge about weather, such as knowing the different basic types of weather (rain, snow, sunny, cloudy) to begin working with this lesson. Advanced learners understand basic weather terminology and already have a good understanding of qualitative observations. They are ready to move to quantitative observations. **Materials:** Materials to represent the various data that will be collected, such as pictures, cut-outs, paper, markers, and an outside thermometer.	
	Typical Learners	**Advanced Learners**
	Essential Question: How do we find patterns in our weather?	
Standard: 　K-ESS2-1. Use and share observations of local weather conditions to describe patterns over time. *Clarification Statement:* Examples of qualitative observations could include descriptions of the weather (e.g., sunny, cloudy, rainy, and warm); examples of quantitative observations could include numbers of sunny, windy, and rainy days in a month. Examples of patterns could include that it is usually cooler in the morning than in the afternoon and the number of sunny days versus cloudy days in different months. *Assessment Boundary:* Assessment of quantitative observations limited to whole numbers and relative measures such as warmer/cooler.	**Directions:** Have students come together in a semicircle around a large calendar that is visible to all. Explain to students that they will be acting like scientists, particularly meteorologists. Introduce the idea of meteorology and meteorologists by reading a book such as *Geoffrey Groundhog Predicts the Weather* (Koscielniak, 1998). Explain (and be sure the students understand) the terms "temperature" and "precipitation". Explain that they will be observing, recording, and sharing representations of our weather. Let students help choose pictures to represent temperatures and precipitation (e.g., a drop for rain, a paper snowflake for snow). Begin by having students look outside and determine if it is sunny, cloudy, rainy, or snowy. Then determine temperature—hot, cold, warm, very cold, and so on. 　Have a different child place the appropriate symbols on the calendar each day. At the end of the month, have students identify patterns, such as "the *continued*	**Directions:** Students will follow the typical learner lesson but substitute this book, *The Kids' Book of Weather Forecasting* (Breen & Friestad, 2008). Students will continue with the typical lesson, but at the end of the month they will work as a group to organize the data, making pictographs of the morning and afternoon temperatures, the cloudy days, rainy days, sunny days, and snowy days. They should be able to answer quantitative questions, such as: Did we have more sunny days or more cloudy days? When was the temperature higher, in the morning or afternoon? Were there changes in patterns (e.g., most days the noon temperature was hotter, but on one occasion it was cooler)?

Grade K: Earth's Systems, *continued*	
	temperature was cooler in the morning than after lunch." Students may take the symbols off of the calendar and use them to form pictographs to assist with finding patterns. Ask students: How did we act like meteorologists?
Implementation	The teacher has determined by preassessment, observation, or formative assessment which students are ready for the advanced learning experience. The teacher will need to form a group or groups of three or four depending on the number of advanced learners. Because the learners read different books, if there is only one teacher, one group may have to work on an anchoring activity while the other listens to the book; then the activities are reversed.
Crosscutting Concept(s)	**Patterns:** Patterns in the natural and human designed world can be observed, used to describe phenomena, and used as evidence.

Grade 3 Earth's Systems	Teacher Information: Typical learners should have the background knowledge about basic weather concepts and how to make charts and graphs to begin working with this lesson; advanced learners already have a good understanding of basic weather concepts and are ready to work with a more complex lesson.	
	Typical Learners	Advanced Learners
	Essential Questions: How do meteorologists predict the weather?	
Standard(s): 3-ESS2-1. Represent data in tables and graphical displays to describe typical weather conditions expected during a particular season. *Clarification Statement:* Examples of data at this grade level could include average temperature, precipitation, and wind direction. *Assessment Boundary:* Assessment of graphical displays is limited to pictographs and bar graphs. Assessment does not include climate change.	Directions: Divide students into groups of three or four and provide them with 4 weeks of temperature (morning, noon, evening), precipitation and wind direction data. Have the groups organize the data using charts or graphs. Have students analyze their data to determine patterns that they notice based on their data. Ask students to identify any patterns they have found (e.g., when the wind changes, there is a temperature change; it is warmer during the day than at night; etc.). Based on the day-to-day patterns and the long-term patterns, ask students to predict what they think the weather will be for the next 5 days. Have students support their conclusions with data.	Directions: Ask students to look at a weather report on television and note how the meteorologist reports the weather. Ask students what they observed while viewing the weather report on TV or if they have seen the weather forecast in the daily newspaper. Ask students, "How do the meteorologists represent the forecast on TV and/or in the newspaper? Why do you think meteorologists use maps to show the weather forecast?" Tell students they are going to learn how to read and create weather maps. Hand out weather maps to each student. (Use maps from the newspaper, forecasting websites, or other sources.) Ask students to look at the map. Encourage them to make observations about the map and to ask questions about it. You may want to write students' observations and questions on the board or on chart paper. Ask students: 1. What do you notice about the weather map? 2. What questions do you have about the map? 3. Do you notice any patterns? *continued*

Grade 3: Earth's Systems, *continued*	
	Provide access to 5-day weather forecasts and allow students to track the changes in weather from one particular city or location in the United States. Have students pair up to compare the weather from their different locations. Have them look for patterns in the weather over time by tracking changes in temperature, precipitation, wind direction, and cloud formation. Lead students in a discussion of the patterns they have found (e.g., when the wind changes direction, there is a change in temperature; clouds change with the type of weather we are having; etc.) Have them support their conclusions.
Implementation	The teacher will need to gather (or have students gather) the necessary 4 weeks of weather data for the typical learning experience. For the advanced learner activities, the teacher will need blank maps of the U.S. with the states outlined and computers available for students to have access to 5-day forecasts.
Crosscutting Concepts	**Patterns:** Patterns of change can be used to make predictions.
Science and Engineering Practices	**Analyzing and Interpreting Data:** Analyzing data in grades 3–5 builds on K–2 experiences and progresses to introducing quantitative approaches to collecting data and conducting multiple trials of qualitative observations. When possible and feasible, digital tools should be used. Representing data in tables and various graphical displays (bar graphs, pictographs, and/or pie charts) reveals patterns that indicate relationships.

Middle School (6–8) Earth's Systems	Teacher Information: Typical learners should have a good understanding of mean, median, mode, and range and the ability to graph. Advanced learners should understand these concepts and be able to apply them to more complex data.	
	Typical Learners	Advanced Learners
	Essential Questions: What are the patterns or trends in our weather? What kinds of questions can we ask when looking at data?	
Standard(s): MS-ESS2-5. Collect data to provide evidence for how the motions and complex interactions of air masses results in changes in weather conditions. *Clarification Statement:* Emphasis is on how air masses flow from regions of high pressure to low pressure, causing weather (defined by temperature, pressure, humidity, precipitation, and wind) at a fixed location to change over time, and how sudden changes in weather can result when different air masses collide. Emphasis is on how weather can be predicted within probabilistic ranges. Examples of data can be provided to students (e.g., weather maps, diagrams, and visualizations) or obtained through *continued*	Directions: Go to the website http://www.easie-mmsa.org/docs/Data/DataGraphingLesson.pdf. Please read "Implementation" first. The learning experience for the typical learner will start on p. 9 with an introduction to data and graph construction. Continue following the guide to Number 6, p. 11. If computers are available for class use, include Number 7, creating a graph using a computer. If not, lead a discussion about how scientists collect weather data (Number 8). Evaluate student understanding using either Handouts 5 and 6 or the assessment found at the website. This assessment may need to be modified for typical learners based on the needs of particular classrooms.	Directions: Go to the same website as the one used in the learning experience for typical learners. Advanced learners will enter the learning experience at Number 8, p. 11, "How scientists collect weather data." It might be helpful to have these students form small groups of three or four. They will continue with Numbers 9 and 10, which involve understanding and interpreting buoy data from the Gulf of Maine (The teacher should review other options on p. 15 that allow more depth and complexity in these activities). After a group discussion in Number 10, have them work on an enrichment lesson, Adopt a Buoy, at the following webpage: http://www.easie-mmsa.org/docs/Enrichment/AdoptABuoy.pdf. Students wishing to take this topic into greater depth could choose the activity Explore Geostationary Operational Environmental Satellite, p. 14. Evaluate student understanding using the assessment found at the website.

Middle School (6–8): Earth's Systems, *continued*

laboratory experiments (such as with condensation). *Assessment Boundary:* Assessment does not include recalling the names of cloud types or weather symbols used on weather maps or the reported diagrams from weather.	
Implementation	Specific instructions for this lesson are found at http://www.easie-mmsa.org/docs/Data/DataGraphing Lesson.pdf. All directions, background information, and handouts are available free to download. This is an introductory unit in which students collect graph and interpret weather data. The main goal is for students to work with and make meaning from real-world data. Students will gather, communicate, interpret, analyze, and evaluate data from a variety of sources. The entire learning experience takes about five class periods, but the teacher will make decisions about actual lesson content based on the needs of the students in the classroom. Not everyone will complete all activities. The teacher might find the Weather and Climate unit helpful.
Crosscutting Concepts	**Cause and Effect:** Cause and effect relationships may be used to predict phenomena in natural or de-signed systems.
Science and Engineering Practices	**Planning and Carrying Out Investigations:** Planning and carrying out investigations in grades 6–8 builds on K–5 experiences and progresses to include investigations that use multiple variables and provide evidence to support explanations or solutions. Collect data to produce data to serve as the basis for evidence to answer scientific questions or test design solutions under a range of conditions.

Note: Learning experiences adapted from *Earth As a System Is Essential: Seasons and the Seas*, by Maine Mathematics and Science Alliance (MMSA), 2011, Augusta, ME: MMSA. Copyright 2011 by MMSA. Adapted with permission.

Grade K
Interdependent Relationships in Ecosystems: Animals, Plants, and Their Environment

Teacher Information: Typical learners will be given a hypothesis and be given directions to set up their experiments. Advanced learners will construct their own hypothesis based on the understanding that was demonstrated through the preassessment. Anchor activities can be set up in the classroom for students to engage in when the teacher is working with the other group. For example, in one anchor, students may be asked to draw or find pictures of plants and animals—on the computer, in magazines, or a preset folder of pictures—that live in a variety of environments: the desert, the tundra, the ocean, or the rainforest. Students will determine what plants and animals need to survive.

Materials: This lesson requires seeds, soil, individual planters, pictures of plants and animals and the book: *Why Living Things Need Food* by Daniel Nunn (2012).

Typical Learners	Advanced Learners
Essential Question: What do plants and animals need to survive?	
Directions: Divide students into groups and assign each a hypothesis: I think a plant needs light to survive; I think a plant needs water to survive; or I think a plant needs soil to survive.	**Directions:** Students will construct a hypothesis about what plants need and hypothesize about any one need that may be more important than the others.
Explain to students how they will conduct an experiment to test their hypothesis by setting up four experiments. The "light" group will place plants in three differently lit areas: near a window, in an area of the room that does not get direct sunlight, and covered with a brown bag in a closet.	With teacher guidance and questioning, students will design an experiment that will test their hypothesis and will design and keep an observational drawing journal.
The "soil" group will use sand, soil, and a mix of both.	If students have not previously had experiences developing a hypothesis, a discussion may take place first. Explain to students that scientists are always asking themselves questions and try to answer their own questions by developing experiments and investigations. First, scientists must come up with a hypothesis. A hypothesis is an explanation or assumption about why something happens.
The "water" group will keep one plant watered daily, another only when needed, and the last watered only on the first day of the experiment.	
Students will keep an observational drawing	
continued	*continued*

Standard(s):

K-LS1-1. Use observations to describe patterns of what plants and animals (including humans) need to survive. *Clarification Statement:* Examples of patterns could include that animals need to take in food but plants do not; the different kinds of food needed by different types of animals; the requirement of plants to have light; and that all living things need water.

Grade K: Interdependent Relationships in Ecosystems, *continued*

journal. Over time, students will compare findings and collaborate to determine which of these factors are most needed.

After experiments are set up (after a few class periods), summarize with students the three things that plants need: water, light, and soil. Then pose the following question for discussion: What do animals need to survive? With a partner, students can brainstorm ideas and write or draw the things that they believe animals need to survive. If needed, prompt them to think of the pets that they may have and ways they take care of that pet.

A classroom pet is also a great way for students to observe what animals need.

Gather a variety of pictures of plants and animals for a compare/contrast experience with the students. Using cording (macramé cording works well) of two different colors, set up two separate circles on the floor area. Label one circle "needs water," label the other circle, "does not need water." Students will sort the pictures to discover that both plants and animals need water.

Change the labels on the circles to: "needs sunlight" and "does not need sunlight." Do the same task as described above. Continue on labeling the circles: needs soil/does not need soil and needs food/does not need food.

continued

Ask students:
1. What do you think is the most important thing that a plant needs?
2. What would happen if the plant did not get any of it?
3. With your group, come up with a hypothesis that you believe is true about the most important thing a plant needs.

Ask students to create a scientific experiment and investigation that will test their hypothesis. Allow students to discuss ideas among themselves and to generate a list of materials that they will need and directions explaining how to put the experiment together. (If they have a science journal, they can record ideas in it.)

Students will construct the experiment and create a way to collect their observations/data over a period of time. Students will then communicate findings to class.

Once experiments are under way, begin introducing what animals need to survive. Pose the following question to the students: What do animals need to survive? A teacher-facilitated discussion will follow. Record all of the students' ideas on the board, chart paper, or projection device.

Ask students to identify the things that both animals and plants need to survive. After this discussion,

continued

Grade K: Interdependent Relationships in Ecosystems, *continued*		
	This strategy will help students discover the things that only plants need, only animals need, and the things that both plants and animals need. Ask students to draw a plant and animal and list all of things they need to survive.	focus on one thing that only animals need: food. Pose the following question: Do all animals need the same kind of food? Read the book: *Why Living Things Need Food* by Daniel Nunn (2012). Through the discussion and reading, students discover the things that only plants need, only animals need, and the things that both plants and animals need. Ask students to draw a plant and animal and list all of things they need to survive.
Implementation	The class will complete an open-ended preassessment about what plants and animals need to survive. Students will illustrate and/or respond to questions about the needs of all living things. Students with knowledge and/or interest and motivation will be part of the advanced learner experience. Anchor activities will be available as a management tool for two instructional groups. Teachers will monitor groups as experiments are set up and data is recorded. Students who demonstrate complete or partial understanding can be part of the advanced learner experience.	
Crosscutting Concepts	**Patterns:** Patterns in the natural and human designed world can be observed and used as evidence.	
Science and Engineering Practices	**Analyzing and Interpreting Data:** Analyzing data in grades K–2 builds on prior experiences and progresses to collecting, recording, and sharing observations. Use observations (firsthand or from media) to describe patterns in the natural world in order to answer scientific questions.	

Grade 3 Inheritance and Variation of Traits: Life Cycles and Traits	**Teacher Information:** The learning experience will allow the advanced learner to discover patterns that are inherent in life cycles. Anchor activities can include a class library with various books on the subject. **Materials:** This lesson requires a variety of fruit seeds and access to research.	
	Typical Learners	**Advanced Learners**
	Essential Question: How do we know that life cycles of plants and animals have similar features and predictable patterns?	
Standard(s): **3-LS1-1. Develop models to describe that organisms have unique and diverse life cycles but all have in common birth, growth, reproduction, and death.** *Clarification Statement:* Changes organisms go through during their life form a pattern. *Assessment Boundary:* Assessment of plant life cycles is limited to those of flowering plants. Assessment does not include details of human reproduction.	**Directions:** Students will examine and discuss similarities and differences in a variety of fruit seeds. Ask students to visualize and communicate what would happen to each seed if they each get everything they need: soil, water, sun, nutrients. Show the students the *From Seed to Flower* video at the following website: http://www.teachersdomain. org/resource/tdc02.sci.life.colt.plantsgrow/. Have the students write some questions with partners about the video. Include questions about what was observed as well as things they want to learn more about. Share questions with the class. Students should determine ways to gather more information in order to answer questions that are posed. Students can use resources to answer posed questions. Students will be given guidance for germinating and growing some of the seeds. Observational journals will be kept. Show students the *Complete Life Cycle of the Monarch Butterfly* video on YouTube: http://www.youtube. com/watch?v=7AUeM8Mbalk. *continued*	**Directions:** With the teacher as facilitator, discuss how the life cycles of plants are the same or different from the life cycles of animals. It is important to note that the teacher is part of the discussion, not the leader. A question can be posed initially that will cause students to wonder about similarities and differences in life cycles. Students collaboratively create an original, unique visual representation of the similarities and differences. Students share the visual representation. Hypothesize about possible patterns that may exist in the life cycles of plants and animals. Students will collaborate and plan for germinating and growing a variety of seeds. Observational journals will be kept. Determine ways to discover and record any patterns that emerge when observing the life cycles of a variety of plants. (e.g., evergreen trees, flowering plants, etc.) and animals (e.g., fish, mammals, vertebrates, etc.). Students should record findings and develop an appropriate graphic organizer to communicate *continued*

Grade 3: Inheritance and Variation of Traits, *continued*

	Arrange the students in small groups to respond to the following question in a whole–class discussion or small–group discussion: How is the life cycle of plants the same or different from the life cycle of animals?	data. An example might be a compare/contrast chart or use of data sharing software. At the end of the learning sequence, students can compare and contrast the life cycle of the plants to the life cycle of animals.
Implementation	The class will complete a preassessment that will capture their knowledge about the main stages in the life cycle of a flowering plant. This could include labeling a diagram of a flowering plant and filling in a cyclical graphic organizer of the life cycle of the plant. Students should also respond to an open–ended question asking them to describe the life cycle of an animal. Students who demonstrate complete or partial understanding can be part of the advanced learner experience.	
Crosscutting Concepts	**Patterns:** Similarities and differences in patterns can be used to sort and classify natural phenomena. Patterns of change can be used to make predictions.	
Science and Engineering Practices	**Analyzing and Interpreting Data:** Analyzing data in grades 3–5 builds on K–2 experiences and progresses to introducing quantitative approaches to collecting data and conducting multiple trials of qualitative observations. When possible and feasible, digital tools should be used. Represent data in tables and various graphical displays (bar graphs, pictographs, and/or pie charts) to reveal patterns that indicate relationships. **Engaging in Argument From Evidence:** Engaging in argument from evidence in grades 3–5 builds on K–2 experiences and progresses to critiquing the scientific explanations or solutions proposed by peers by citing relevant evidence about the natural and designed world(s). Make a claim about the merit of a solution to a problem by citing relevant evidence about how it meets the criteria and constraints of the problem.	

Middle School Growth, Development, and Reproduction of Organisms	**Teacher Information:** Typical learners will focus on ways that environmental factors can affect the growth of an organism. Advanced learners will go deeper into the genetic factors that affect the growth of an organism. Environmental factors can be compacted for this group of students.	
	Typical Learners	**Advanced Learners**
	Essential Question: How do environmental and genetic factors affect the growth of organisms?	
Standard(s): **MS-LS1-5. Construct a scientific explanation based on evidence for how environmental and genetic factors influence the growth of organisms.** *Clarification Statement:* Examples of local environmental conditions could include availability of food, light, space, and water. Examples of genetic factors could include large breed cattle and species of grass affecting growth of organisms. Examples of evidence could include drought decreasing plant growth, fertilizer increasing plant growth, different varieties of plant seeds growing at different rates in different conditions, and fish growing larger in large ponds than they do in small ponds. *Assessment Boundary:* Assessment does not include genetic mechanisms, gene regulation, or biochemical processes.	**Directions:** Ask students to brainstorm environmental factors that may affect the growth of plants and/or animals. Anticipated responses include: temperature, soil, supply of nutrients, moisture, weather, sun, amount of space, and availability of food sources. Write these responses on cards or post where students can see them. These factors can be referred to throughout the lesson sequence as needed. Provide students with directions for setting up an experiment that will examine environmental or genetic factors of organisms. Environmental factors: Several testable questions and experiment ideas are provided on the *Science Made Simple* website: http://www.sciencemadesimple.com/botany_plant_projects.html Questions include: 1. How do different conditions affect the speed at which fruit and vegetables ripen? 2. What happens when you grow sweet potatoes next to other plants? 3. Does the amount of room a plant has for roots make a difference in how big a plant will grow? *continued*	**Directions:** The teacher facilitates a discussion about genetic factors that may affect the growth of plants and/or animals. Begin with the question, "Are people born good or do they learn to be good?" Ask students to base their discussion on evidence, which may draw out misconceptions. Ask, "How do genetics affect humans?" Anticipated responses include: height, hair and eye color, cancer/diseases, and addiction. Teachers may also graph genetic features that each child has: widow's peak, rolling tongue, etc. Ask students, "How can genetics affect the growth of a plant?" In small groups, students will chose one or more of the genetic factors that they brainstormed and design an experiment that proves or disproves a negative or positive effect on growth. Their arguments must be based on evidence. Using examples such as dog breeds and hybrid vegetables, engage students in a discussion and readings about how these breeds and variety of hybrid fruits and vegetables came to be. Students will choose a plant or animal to study and prepare a presentation *continued*

Middle School: Growth, Development, and Reproduction of Organisms, *continued*	
	4. What affect does the brightness of light have on the growth rate of a plant? **Genetic factors:** A possible experiment that can be used to address genetics is using fruit flies. Background and experiment ideas can be found at the following website: http://www.unc.edu/depts/our/hhmi/hhmi-ft_learning_modules/fruitflymodule/.	that highlights the genetic and environmental influences that played a part in the development of the organism.
Implementation	The class will complete a preassessment that will capture their knowledge about using evidence for how environmental and genetic factors affect the growth of organisms. They may respond to questions such as: What environmental factors affect the growth of organisms? What genetic factors affect the growth of organisms? Students who demonstrate understanding of environmental factors but not genetic factors can be part of the advanced learner group.	
Crosscutting Concepts	**Cause and Effect:** Phenomena may have more than one cause, and some cause and effect relationships in systems only can be described using probability.	
Science and Engineering Practices	**Constructing Explanations and Designing Solutions:** Constructing explanations and designing solutions in grades 6–8 builds on K–5 experiences and progresses to include constructing explanations and designing solutions supported by multiple sources of evidence consistent with scientific knowledge, principles, and theories. Construct a scientific explanation based on valid and reliable evidence obtained from sources (including the students' own experiments) and the assumption that theories and laws that describe the natural world operate today as they did in the past and will continue to do so in the future. **Obtaining, Evaluating, and Communicating Information:** Obtaining, evaluating, and communicating information in grades 6–8 builds on K–5 experiences and progresses to evaluating the merit and validity of ideas and methods. Gather, read, and synthesize information from multiple appropriate sources and assess the credibility, accuracy, and possible bias of each publication and methods used, and describe how they are supported or not supported by evidence.	

Differentiating Assessments to Encourage Higher Level Reasoning

Although grade-level performance expectations are identified in the NGSS, teachers must also consider how differentiation of classroom assessments can be tailored to support the ongoing development of each student's science abilities in order to meet gifted students' unique academic needs.

In science, curriculum may be modified to include more advanced, above-grade-level content (more difficult material, greater depth of exploration), level of inquiry, and more rigorous problems and projects that challenge students to stretch beyond their current level of performance. Assessments must be able to accurately gauge the growth of the advanced learner. Thus, product-based assessment is a crucial approach in differentiation. These product-based assessments should include authentic, unfamiliar problem solving and problem posing for which students keep portfolios of exemplary work and research projects. Student interests should be taken into consideration for at least some of these assessment problems and projects.

The NGSS often include an "assessment boundary" within a particular standard so that teachers will know the level of knowledge and understanding that is expected for that particu-

---

3-LS3 Heredity: Inheritance and Variation of Traits

Students who demonstrate understanding can:

3-LS3-1. Analyze and interpret data to provide evidence that plants and animals have traits inherited from parents and that variation of these traits exists in a group of similar organisms.

[Assessment Boundary: Assessment does not include genetic mechanisms of inheritance and prediction of traits. Assessment is limited to non-human examples]

Figure 4. Disciplinary core idea for grade 3, Life Science, Standard 3-1.

---

lar standard. In Figure 4, the disciplinary core idea is for grade 3, Life Science, Standard 3-1. The assessment boundary indicates assessment does not include genetic mechanisms of inheritance and prediction of traits, and human examples will not be used. For example, instead of discussing meiosis and mitosis and the incidents of chromosomal damage that may cause a particular abnormality, the discussion may be limited to factors such as malnutrition that may cause abnormalities. Because these boundaries are for the typical student, teachers may extend the boundary for gifted and advanced learners. In this example, gifted students may go further in-depth on the topic of heredity and study the genetic mechanism of inheritance, including genetic inheritance in humans.

Ongoing Assessments

Ongoing formative and summative assessment should be embedded in classroom instruction using strategies such as entry and exit slips and evaluation of student work during class. It is important to include challenging problems that can be solved on a variety of levels in a variety of different ways and that encourage extensions, creativity, and higher level reasoning to allow students to display and develop their science talents. If standardized tests are used, they must have a high enough ceiling (i.e., concepts and content above grade level) to provide students the opportunity to exhibit scientific expertise that goes beyond grade level.

Computer-assisted assessment that automatically adjusts the level of questions based on student responses might be used to identify growth and monitor continuous progress.

Assessing Specific Skills

Assessment of spatial abilities, such as the ability to manipulate three-dimensional objects (e.g., models of molecules), and scientific creativity are also important for the development of STEM innovators. Fields such as engineering, surgery, chemistry, physics, architecture, and many more require that students have highly developed spatial reasoning abilities, which are often overlooked in science programs for the development of scientific gifts and talents.

In addition to spatial abilities, the NGSS emphasize scientific inquiry and discourse in the science and engineering practices embedded in each standard. The NRC (2012) noted that:

Standards and performance expectations that are aligned to the framework must take into account that students cannot fully understand scientific and engineering ideas without engaging in the practices of inquiry and the discourses by which such ideas are developed and refined. At the same time, they cannot learn or show competence in practices except in the context of specific content. (p. 218)

Hence, engaging in scientific inquiry is expected of all students K–12. Figure 5 shows a rubric that may be used for assessing students' ability to design a scientific investigation. Because there are two forms, it may be used as a pre- or postassessment. Students are given the prompt and asked to design a fair test. The directions for Form A are as follows: Tell how you would test this question: Do bees like diet cola? Be as scientific as you can as you write about your test. Write down the steps you would

Fowler Science Process Skills Assessment
Pretest/Posttest Scoring Sheet

Name of Student _____ School _____

Score one point on student paper for each item incorporated into design. Score two points if more than one subitem is listed for a specific item.

Pre		Post
	plans to practice **SAFETY**	
	states **PROBLEM** or **QUESTION**	
	PREDICTS outcome or **HYPOTHESIZES**	
	lists more than **3 STEPS**	
	arranges steps in **SEQUENTIAL** order	
	lists **MATERIALS** needed	
	plans to **REPEAT TESTING** and tells a reason	
	other items listed by student but not on list	
	DEFINES the terms of the experiment: "attracted to," "likes," "bees," "diet cola" **DEFINES** the terms of the experiment: "attracted to," "likes," "earthworms," "light"	
	plans to **OBSERVE**	
	plans to **MEASURE** (e.g., linear distance between bees, and/or cola, number of bees, time involved) plans to **MEASURE:** (e.g., linear distance between worms, and/ or light, number of worms, time involved, amount of light)	
	plans **DATA COLLECTION:** graph or table, note taking, labels	
	states plan for **INTERPRETING DATA:** comparing data; looking for patterns in data; in terms of definitions used; in terms of previously known information	
	states plan for making **CONCLUSION BASED ON DATA** (e.g., time to notice drinks; bees may not be hungry; distances to sodas are equal; time involved for two samples is equal; temperature, light, wind, etc. are equal) states plan for making **CONCLUSION BASED ON DATA** (e.g., time to notice light; distances to light and shade are equal; time involved for two samples is equal; temperature, wind, etc. are equal)	
	plans to **CONTROL VARIABLES** (e.g., bees not hungry; bees choose diet or regular soda; distances set equally; amounts of soda equal; number of bees tested are equal; temperature, light, wind, etc. are equal) plans to **CONTROL VARIABLES** (e.g., worms choose dark or light; distances set equally; number of worms tested are equal; time involved is equal; temperature, wind, etc. are equal)	

Pretest score:_____ Name of rater:_____ Date:_____

Posttest score: _____ Name of rater:_____ Date:_____

Source: Fowler, M. (1990). The diet cola test. *Science Scope, 13*(4), 32–34

Figure 5. Assessment rubric. From "The Diet Cola Test," by M. Fowler, 1990, *Science Scope, 13*, p. 32–34. Copyright 1990 by the National Science Teachers Association. Adapted with permission.

take to find out if bees like diet cola. For Form B, substitute the question, Do earthworms like light?

There are numerous types of assessments and equally many reasons for assessment; thus, we should proceed with caution and consider the reason for giving the assessment. If the assessment is used to determine participants in higher level opportunities, care must be taken to be as inclusive as possible and not to use the assessment as a gatekeeper. That is, entry into advanced classes or learning opportunities should be based on a variety of factors, not just one assessment. In many instances, self-selection for advanced programs can be used quite successfully, assuming that courses and programs are not watered down for unprepared students.

If the assessment is used to determine what was learned in the classroom, we need to provide differentiated assessments for differentiated lessons. The assessments used for typical students will stay within the NGSS assessment boundaries, but assessments for advanced learners may go beyond the boundaries if their learning experiences were more advanced. In each case, the assessment mirrors what was taught and how the students interacted with the lessons.

Talent Trajectory: Creating Pathways to Excellence in Science

As noted in *Preparing the Next Generation of STEM Innovators*, "The long-term prosperity of our Nation will increasingly rely on talented and motivated individuals who will comprise the vanguard of scientific and technological innovations; every student in America deserves the opportunity to achieve his or her full potential" (NSB, 2010, p. v). Educators need to increase the number and levels of these promising science students and not limit the numbers of students in advanced science and specialized STEM programs. Whether students plan to enter a STEM field in a career anywhere from astronaut to zoologist or simply want to become well-informed citizens who can make sense of the world, recognize patterns, make generalizations, test conjectures, make and defend logical decisions, and critique the reasoning of others, science is critical to their development. Some of the characteristics of thinking like a scientist that teachers should encourage and develop in themselves as well as their students can be harvested from the eight practices of science and engineering from the *Framework for K–12 Science Education* (NRC, 2012):

- scientific curiosity, asking questions and defining problems;

- analyzing and interpreting data;
- engaging in constructive arguments from evidence;
- communicating information;
- creativity and innovation;
- a growth mindset with confidence in their abilities to learn science on a deeper level;
- willingness to take risks and increasingly difficult challenges; and
- perseverance in the face of failure.

Both Acceleration and Time for Exploration

Preparation of high-level STEM students should not be rushed. Appropriate pacing for our top students should include not only acceleration, but also time for our students to experience the joy of investigating rich concepts in depth and applying innovative scientific reasoning and justification to a variety of scientific, mathematical, engineering, and other problems. They should have engaging, problem-based learning that requires students to grapple with scientific challenges in order to deepen their understanding of complex concepts (NAGC, 2008). There should be a seamless articulation from elementary to middle to high school, where courses are carefully planned and there is little repetition of courses or content within the courses. This should include flexibility in scheduling, location, seat time, and other potential impediments to ensure that students make continuous progress throughout the K–12 programs in those areas that hold great interest and appeal. For example, students who are interested in science and preparing for STEM careers should have opportunities to take math and science every year of high school from highly motivated teachers. There should be widespread availability of specialized STEM schools, programs, or classes for students from elementary through high school to fuel their passions and give them the preparation necessary to move ahead.

Many students who are advanced or gifted in STEM should be prepared for rigorous high school courses by eighth grade or earlier—perhaps through a carefully constructed, compacted, or telescoped curriculum—and should be encouraged and have the opportunity to do so. The National Science Board (2004) warns that algebra is a gatekeeping course, and students who do not take it in eighth grade have a more difficult time completing the necessary STEM courses required to enter higher education as STEM majors.

Following the first 3 years of high school physics, chemistry, and biology, a menu of science course options should be available. These options for advanced courses might include advanced, honors, or AP courses in biology, chemistry, physics, and specialized courses such as organic chemistry or microbiology. Courses should be designed to be challenging, engaging, and relevant, preparing and exciting students about their futures in college and careers. These courses may be provided at the high school, online, or through dual enrollment at a nearby college or university.

Appendix J of the NGSS provides three different course maps that are models of different ways to map the performance expectations of grades 6–8 and 9–12 onto courses: the conceptual progressions model, the science domain model, and the modified science domain model. There is a discussion of benefits and challenges to each; however, these are course maps for students on a typical trajectory, not a talent trajectory. There are no suggestions for talent trajectories for advanced students in the NGSS or the *Framework for K–12 Science Education*, but as in mathematics, advanced and talented science students need access to advanced classes earlier and more often than typical learners.

Purposeful planning should occur for those students who decide after middle school that they are interested in taking advanced science such as AP and International Baccalaureate (IB) courses before leaving high school. Additional opportunities for acceleration should be available. For example:

- allowing students to take two science courses simultaneously;

- allowing students in schools with block scheduling to take a science course in both semesters of the same academic year;
- offering summer courses that are designed to provide the equivalent experience of a full-year course in all regards;
- creating different compaction ratios, including 4 years of high school content into 3 years beginning in ninth grade;
- creating hybrid courses; and
- allowing students to participate in programs such as the AP Cambridge Capstone Program (http://aphighered. collegeboard.org/exams/cambridge-capstone).

These recommendations are more in line with the acceleration research literature and position statements in gifted education that suggest intellectually talented youth achieve at an impressively high level if they receive an appropriately challenging education (Benbow & Stanley, 1996; Colangelo et al., 2004; Swiatek & Benbow, 1991, 1992). The National Association for Gifted Children's (2004) position statement on acceleration described "grade skipping, telescoping, early entrance into kindergarten or college, credit by examination, and acceleration in content areas" as research-based options and concluded by stating, "Highly able students with capability and motivation to succeed in placements beyond traditional age/grade parameters should be provided the opportunity to enroll in appropriate classes and educational settings" (para. 7).

Extracurricular Opportunities

Schools that may not have access to an array of science course options for advanced and gifted students may want to consider connecting with mentors in the community or providing distance learning and online courses, such as those offered by the Education Program for Gifted Youth at Stanford, Johns Hopkins Center for Talented Youth, Duke Center for Talented Youth,

Northwestern Center for Talent Development, Carnegie-Mellon Institute for Talented Elementary and Secondary Students, and other programs.

It is vital that educators develop the passion as well as the expertise, motivation, and creativity of their most promising science students. There are a number of extracurricular opportunities that can enhance this development. These opportunities should be in addition to, not in place of, engaging and challenging K–12 curricular science programs. These extracurricular opportunities might include:

- science clubs and circles;
- mentorships and apprenticeships;
- math, science, and STEM competitions;
- conducting authentic scientific research;
- undertaking engineering design challenges; and
- online or other electronic experiences.

All students, including high-ability learners, should have access to pathways to excellence in science. Currently, many student opportunities exist in the form of out-of-school enrichment activities (e.g., science/math clubs, competitions, summer camps). To increase opportunities for talent development, acceleration, ample time, and advanced course matriculation must be considered (NSB, 2010). Creating multiple pathways that work in concert as synchronized education rather than as stand-alone options increases the likelihood for student success in the STEM disciplines.

Implementing the NGSS With Various Program Models in Gifted Education

The models of delivery are largely not addressed in the NGSS, allowing teachers and schools to implement services based on the needs of gifted students with the NGSS as a basis. Although gifted program design and delivery will be informed by these standards, programs and services for the gifted should be largely guided by assessment data about the abilities of students, as well as by best practices for serving them in each of the core subject areas.

As gifted program service models vary, so do the implementation implications for the NGSS. Gifted students receive services within heterogeneous settings, cluster-grouped classrooms, pull-out models, self-contained classrooms, and specialized schools.

Flexible Grouping in the Regular Classroom

As the NGSS authors acknowledge in the NGSS Appendix D (Achieve, Inc., 2013a), the standards are limited in nature when addressing the specific needs of gifted and talented students; therefore, it is imperative that teachers modify learning experiences for these students. For teachers of gifted and high-potential learners served in the heterogeneous, general education classroom with flexible grouping, the NGSS can serve as benchmarks for what all students should know, although educators should be careful not to limit curriculum for high-ability students based on the foundational expectations that would be provided to general education learners. In fact, those who are advanced may show mastery of content standards much sooner than other learners.

To address the curricular needs of gifted and high-potential students, teachers can differentiate curriculum through using pre- and formative assessments, compacting or accelerating the curriculum, posing progressively more complex issues, adjusting or replacing texts according to each student's reading level and interest, modifying science processes according to those previously mastered, and pacing instruction according to individual rates of learning. The need for authentically challenging activities for advanced students in science is not to be underestimated, as it links closely with student interest, which ultimately translates to lifelong pursuits in the STEM disciplines.

Cluster Grouping

Cluster grouping involves the placement of gifted and talented learners in a homogenous group based on ability, potential, or achievement. In cluster-grouped classrooms, teachers can use the NGSS as a basis for preassessment of where students are performing and adjust grouping according to students' abilities, interests, and strengths with respect to the varying domains of science. Teachers can group high-ability students flexibly throughout the school day to allow them the opportunity to regularly engage with peers of similar abilities and interests according to individual science skills addressed in the NGSS or by a combination of skills.

Pull-Out Models

Teachers who serve gifted students in pull-out models, where students spend a portion of their school day (or week) in a setting other than their general education classroom, are encouraged to consider how the experiences offered in the pull-out setting offer advanced learning experiences in science that are beyond those that would be provided in the general education classroom. Along with other methods of differentiation, such as providing for greater depth, complexity, and critical thinking opportunities, teachers are encouraged to use ongoing assessment information, including preassessments, to accommodate for the differences in science ability between and among the students in the pull-out program.

Self-Contained

Gifted students who are served throughout the school day with gifted peers in self-contained classrooms engage in a range of science experiences as different content areas are addressed. Although teachers of the gifted in these classrooms use the NGSS as a foundation for setting grade-level expectations, they also consider gifted learners with advanced skills in science who often evidence proficiency in foundational skills early in the school year or at a pace that is faster than general education peers or even their gifted education peers. Thus, appropriate grouping within the self-contained classroom is recommended according to science abilities. The curriculum should be qualitatively different from the curriculum offered to general education students according to the needs of individual students in terms of rate of learning, depth of content, difficulty of products, and complexity of thinking processes.

Special Schools

Special schools for gifted students are available for both elementary and secondary students. In general, the curriculum offered is both accelerated and enriched to provide accommodations for students who can handle work that is significantly more advanced than what is typical for their age mates. Although these

schools serve only students with gifts and talents and the curriculum offerings tend to be advanced, it is still vital that school
personnel go beyond simply using the NGSS for a higher grade
level when creating or aligning curriculum. Keeping in mind the
natural progression of knowledge and skills, specialized schools
must be certain that addressing any gaps in knowledge resulting
from radical acceleration is a priority, particularly when students
are pulled to the specialized school from many different educational settings. Additionally, although students spend time in
specialized schools with their intellectual peers, all gifted students
in any particular class are not alike in their need for a different
pace and differentiation in the complexity of the material being
taught. For example, scientifically advanced students may vary
not only in their scientific abilities (science content knowledge,
concept attainment, science process skills), but also may or may
not be advanced in other content areas. The NGSS is an important tool to use in determining how to accommodate individual
needs within a class not only in science but also in mathematics
and literacy supported by the Common Core State Standards.

Other than specialized schools, most of the programming
options discussed are used primarily at the elementary and middle school levels, but there is no reason that these cannot be used
at the secondary level, too. Because upper-level coursework is
highly specialized, educators may believe that those who take
such courses are advanced to the same degree. Simply because
students are studying advanced chemistry at the 10th-grade level
does not mean that all students in the class are able to handle the
same level of abstraction or can keep up with a fast pace. The
NGSS can be used as a guideline to spur the necessary accommodations by looking across the standards for material to advance
to the next level of learning.

Implications for Professional Learning When Implementing the NGSS

Professional learning is essential for all educators to increase effectiveness and results for students (Learning Forward, 2011). Teachers and content specialists should collaborate in learning communities to identify specific knowledge and skills needed to serve different groups of learners. As schools and school districts adopt and begin using the NGSS, all educators should be involved in a variety of ongoing learning options, including job-embedded professional development to address the needs of gifted and high-potential students. All educators need a repertoire of research-supported strategies to deliberately adapt and modify curriculum, instruction, and assessment within the framework of the NGSS based on the needs of gifted students as well as those with high potential. Professional learning opportunities can also be cross-disciplinary, such as math and science collaboration.

Although the NGSS provide the framework for the learning experiences for all students, gifted educators need focused training that is content-specific for differentiating the standards (VanTassel-Baska et al., 2008). Systematic professional learning will support all educators to adapt, modify, or replace the NGSS based on the needs of the learner. To differentiate effectively for gifted and high-potential learners, all educators need to develop expertise at *designing learning experiences and assessments that are conceptually advanced, challenging, and complex.*

Professional learning for implementing the NGSS for gifted and high-potential learners should focus on evidence-based differentiation and instructional practices as they relate to specific core content. The training should demonstrate how and when to apply acceleration strategies; how to add depth and complexity elements, such as critical thinking, creative thinking, problem solving, and inquiry; and how to develop and encourage innovation, all within the NGSS. In addition to the curriculum adaptation and modification, the professional learning experiences should also demonstrate content-specific ways to design and implement differentiated product-based assessments as well as pre- and postassessments appropriate for advanced students. However, gifted educators are in no way expected to be experts in all content areas; therefore, it is imperative to develop collaborative relations with skilled content specialists to provide knowledgeable advice, content-specific peer coaching services, and pedagogical knowledge while implementing the NGSS.

Examples of Professional Learning Models for Implementing the NGSS

Educators should take an active role in designing learning options to facilitate their learning and improvement of student results (Learning Forward, 2011). Active learning may include any of the following elements:
- discussion and dialogue,
- coaching and modeling,
- demonstration and reflection,
- inquiry and problem solving, and
- tiered model of professional learning experiences (Learning Forward, 2011).

Discussion and dialogue. A professional learning commu‐ nity (PLC) of three to six teachers may agree to work together to improve their practice and student results (Lieberman & Miller, 2008). The PLC would identify specific learning standards for its grade within the NGSS. Through regularly scheduled meet‐ ings, the group of teachers would share ideas on ways to teach the standard, including ideas on differentiation of the learning experiences for advanced learners. The teachers of the PLC would identify strategies from the discussions, implement them in their classrooms, and then share their experiences when the group meets again. Ideally, the PLC would have collaboration and support from a gifted education specialist to provide ideas and resources for studying and practicing effective differentiation for advanced and gifted students.

Coaching and modeling. Learning options can include collaborative relationships such as mentoring or coaching. Specifically, peer coaching as a form of job-embedded profes‐ sional development provides teachers a natural support system that can enhance teacher performance by the privileged sharing of knowledge and expertise through collaboration (Little, 2005). Whether it is the gifted educator serving as a peer coach or the one being coached, the coach may assume various roles, including science content expert, classroom helper, teacher observer, and at times science instructional facilitator (Cotabish & Robinson, 2012; Dailey, Cotabish, & Robinson, 2013).

Demonstration and reflection. Demonstrations are a great way for teachers to learn new practices within authentic contexts. Professional learning leaders (Learning Forward, 2011) can work with teachers to demonstrate differentiation strategies within the NGSS. Examples of this model may include a teacher who is skillfully using preassessment to diagnose science learner readiness and providing differentiated tasks based on the results. The organizer of the professional learning would arrange for teacher-learners to observe the demonstration one or more times, and then practice the strategy in their classrooms. Ultimately the active demonstration strategy is enhanced by reflection of what was learned and how the implementation improved student engagement and performance.

Inquiry and problem solving. Inquiry and problem solving are techniques involving action research by a teacher or team of teachers. In the action research process, teachers examine their own educational practice systematically and carefully using techniques of research. The inquiry conducted by the teacher or team will generate data to inform or change teaching practices. Two of the primary benefits of an action research approach to professional learning is the immediacy and proximity of the inquiry and the teacher's classroom within the expected content of the curriculum. For instance, a teacher or a group of teachers may decide to study the effects of providing differentiated science learning experiences to advanced learners. Research techniques of measurement and consistent implementation would guide the inquiry with base-line assessment data for all students in the intervention, as well as a control group if one is available. The teacher would implement the intervention, differentiated science instruction, over a determined period of time and follow it with posttesting to look for changes in student achievement (within-subjects) or differences compared to the comparison group without the intervention (between-subjects). Frequently, professional learning specialists help teachers develop ideas and data collection techniques for inquiry and problem solving.

Tiered model of professional learning experiences. In a tiered model of professional learning, the school or school district establishes clear expectations for developing expertise in gifted pedagogy and differentiated instruction (Johnsen, Kettler, & Lord, 2011). For gifted education professionals, the model would be built around the NAGC-CEC national standards for gifted education professional development (Kitano, Montgomery, VanTassel-Baska, & Johnsen, 2008). Leaders within the school or school district would develop seminar learning experiences in which teachers would come together to learn differentiation strategies according to these tiered expectations (e.g., novice, intermediate, advanced). Experts in science differentiation would discuss and demonstrate specific ways to differentiate the NGSS across grade levels. As teachers acquire expertise, they gradually move up the tiers from novice to intermediate to expert. As they reach expert levels, they begin to model the expertise and lead seminars with other teachers in their content area. The key ingredient is to provide clear guidelines of the skills expected to develop expertise in differentiating with the NGSS.

Collaboration to
Support Achievement

It cannot be emphasized enough that science teachers and gifted education professionals must collaborate with other educational partners and not "go it alone" in the process of implementing the Next Generation Science Standards on behalf of advanced learners and their talent development process. Gifted educators' roles include direct service and advocacy for the gifted child, including academic, social, and emotional development. It is important to recognize that giftedness impacts the development of the whole child, which involves both external and internal factors. Numerous partners need to be involved in the collaboration process depending on the specific needs and abilities of the child.

First, science content experts must be included in any discussions. When examining trajectories in science, it is critical that experts be involved in the process. Although gifted education specialists have significant training and expertise in strategy instruction, they must partner with science educators who have passion, expertise, and awareness of science trajectories so that students with promise and talent in science receive appropriate levels of instruction that are not tied to age or grade considerations. Domain-specific strengths have different entry points; therefore, it is important to understand trajectories in science so that opportunities for talent development are not missed (Subotnik, Olszewski-Kubilius, & Worrell, 2012).

Second, parents and families must be included in the collaboration process. Although schools and educators play a critical role in the process of talent development, there is an equally important role of outside clubs, competitions, and community opportunities. Parents clearly play a role in mediating the selection and promotion of skills and activities in which students can engage. Parents must be perceived as both a source and a recipient of pertinent information, as well as partners in the educational process.

Third, people from outside entities who promote specific science emphases must be approached as partners in providing opportunities for promising science students. These entities can include online communities, local research centers and laboratories, and colleges and universities. Individuals affiliated with professional organizations might also provide connections to students and are valuable collaborators to facilitate talent development in science.

Fourth, when working with gifted students from diverse and special populations, gifted educators must collaborate with professionals who advocate and provide services for other traditionally underserved students. Educators from special education, English language learner education, and poverty-related programs all play key roles in the development of talent in gifted children who are impacted by other factors within their lives. The National Science Teachers Association encourages an inquiry-based approach that allows for all students to experience success. In an article entitled "Promoting Inclusive Practices in Inquiry-Based Science Classrooms" (Watt, Thierren, Kalderberg, & Taylor, 2013), the authors discussed the importance of explicit instruction within an inquiry-based classroom especially for students with disabilities. "A more structured inquiry approach that utilizes explicit enhancements has been found to be the most effective strategy for instructing students with disabilities" (Therrien, Taylor, Hosp, Kaldenburg, & Gorsh, 2011, p. 41, as cited in Watt, et al. 2013). Providing a balance of instructional support and inquiry-based learning can be a successful combination for students with disabilities who are also advanced or have high potential in science.

Lastly, and very critically, within their roles as gatekeepers and managers of the entire educational process, administrators must be included in discussions of systemic talent development. Rather than making talent development a highly individualistic, ad hoc process, administrators play a key role in systematizing an educational program that can provide progression within the disciplines for talented students.

A Possible Timeline for Locally Adapting the NGSS for Advanced Students

Implementation of the NGSS at the K–12 level encompasses several varied but necessary tasks (see Table 1). For example, the three dimensions: practices, crosscutting concepts, and disciplinary core ideas must be taken together as a way in which educators can develop science practitioners and scientific expertise, not just proficient science students. A first step toward implementation is to become familiar with all of the components of the standards. Second, look at current practices, analyzing them to determine if there are gaps between those and practices that would reflect the NGSS. Next, provide all teachers with professional development that is targeted on best practices in science and with gifted students. Where gaps have been identified, teachers then adjust content, process, products, and assessments to reflect the new science standards, bearing in mind that student outcomes should be aimed at developing expertise. Gather resources and consult with content specialists and gifted education specialists to assist with this realignment. Consider the NAGC Programming Standards (NAGC, 2010) in the realignment process. Make sure the curriculum that is developed is coherent and is focused on the development of concepts, not

Table 1
A Sample Timeline for Implementation of the NGSS

Task	Person(s) Responsible	When
Know and understand the NGSS for the grade level(s) or course(s) you teach.	All school personnel	April–May
Gather evidence to determine the extent to which current practices reflect the standards; identify gaps in practice and or content.	Teacher representatives at each grade level, building level administrators, gifted specialist	June–August
Gather evidence to determine the extent to which current content, process, product, and assessment reflect the content standards; identify gaps in practice and or content.	Teacher representatives at each grade level, building level administrators, gifted specialist, science specialist	September–November
Provide professional development to identify best practices in teaching science and adapting the NGSS for students with gifts and talents.	Gifted specialist, content specialists	December–February
Make adjustments to content, process, product, and assessments to reflect gaps that were identified, deleting curriculum that is not rigorous and does not meet the standards.	All teachers	March–April
Gather resources to assist with realignment to NGSS and to gifted education programming standards.	GT education specialist, building administrator, science specialist, and other necessary personnel	March–April
Provide professional development to prepare all teachers for full implementation of the NGSS for gifted and high-potential students.	GT education specialist, building administrator, science specialist, and other necessary personnel	May–June
Provide ongoing support for full implementation.	GT education specialist, building administrator, science specialist, and other necessary personnel	July–August

add-on activities. There should be strong and clear connections among content, process, product, and assessment. Provide professional development to ensure that school personnel understand the new standards and the changes needed to implement them for gifted and high-potential students.

Resources to Assist With the Implementation Process

There are a variety of resources that can assist university personnel, administrators, and coordinators of gifted programs at state and local levels in implementing the new NGSS for gifted learners, including assessments that measure the depth and breadth of a student's knowledge within a domain of talent development; curriculum units of study that are already differentiated and research-based; instructional strategies that employ the use of higher order thinking skills; and programming options that include appropriate pacing, rigor, innovation, and extended learning beyond the classroom.

The NAGC Programming Standards (2010) should be used as a tool to understand the elements that a differentiated curriculum for the gifted learner would include. For university personnel, it would be helpful to review the gifted education teacher preparation standards (NAGC & CEC, 2006) to see the extent to which there is alignment to the new CCSS.

Below is a sampling of resources that might be considered in implementing the NGSS with gifted students.

Assessment

Johnsen, S. K. (Ed.). (2012). *NAGC pre-K–grade 12 gifted education programming standards: A guide to planning and implementing high-quality services.* Waco, TX: Prufrock Press.

Sulak, T. N., & Johnsen, S. K. (2012). Assessments for measuring student outcomes. In S. K. Johnsen (Ed.), *NAGC Pre-K–grade 12 gifted education programming standards: A guide to planning and implementing high-quality services* (pp. 283–306). Waco, TX: Prufrock Press.

Assessments for measuring the progress of gifted and talented students may be found in the *NAGC Pre-K–Grade 12 Gifted Education Programming Standards: A Guide to Planning and Implementing High-Quality Services* (Johnsen, 2012). Sulak and Johnsen (2012) described informal assessments that might be available without charge and used informally in assessing student outcomes in creativity, critical thinking, curriculum, interests, learning and motivation, and social–emotional areas. They also have identified specific product and performance assessments and other assessments that might be useful in program planning and evaluation. Although many of the assessments do not have technical information, 23 do provide either reliability or validity information.

Robins, J. A., & Jolly, J. L. (2011). Technical information regarding assessment. In S. K. Johnsen (Ed.), *Identifying gifted students: A practical guide* (2nd ed., pp. 75–188). Waco, TX: Prufrock Press.

Information regarding standardized achievement tests may be found in *Identifying Gifted Students: A Practical Guide.* In their chapter, Robins and Jolly provided a list of 28 instruments that are frequently used in the identification of gifted students and their technical qualities. Because many of these assessments are also used to identify students who are above grade level in specific academic areas, they would be appropriate for measuring a gifted student's academic progress.

Curriculum and Instructional Strategies

Carnegie Mellon Institute for Talented Elementary and Secondary Students

Carnegie Mellon Institute for Talented Elementary and Secondary Students (C-MITES) offers resources and links to curricula in mathematics, science, technology, engineering, language arts, and social studies. For more information, visit http:// www.cmu.edu/cmites.

Center for Gifted Education at the College of William & Mary

The Center for Gifted Education at the College of William & Mary has designed curricular units in the areas of mathematics, language arts, science, and social studies that are based on the three dimensions of the Integrated Curriculum Model: advanced content, higher level processes and products, and interdisciplinary concepts, issues, and themes. The materials emphasize a sophistication of ideas, opportunities for extensions, the use of higher order thinking skills, and opportunities for student exploration based on interest. The science curriculum units are geared toward different grade-level clusters, yet can be adapted for use at all levels K–8. Through these units, students experience the work of real science in applying data-handling skills, analyzing information, evaluating results, and learning to communicate their understanding to others. For more information about the William & Mary units, visit the Center for Gifted Education at http://education.wm.edu/centers/cfge/curriculum/index.php.

NGSS Website

The website from the developers of the NGSS (http:// www.nextgenscience.org) provides news about tools that are being developed to support the standards' implementation. For more information, visit http://www.nextgenscience.org/ implementation. Appendix D provides seven case studies that demonstrate ways to implement the NGSS with diverse groups of students. Case Study 7 addresses the learning needs of gifted students: http://nextgenscience.org/appendix-d-case-studies.

U-STARS Plus

U-STARS Plus, a previously funded U.S. Department of Education Jacob K. Javits project, provides *Science and Literature Connections* to explore scientific ideas within literacy instruction time using 32 popular children's books. *Science and Literature Connections* is organized around Bloom's taxonomy to support a range of thinking levels and to scaffold learning. By using these materials, a teacher can create a higher level thinking environment around literature connected with science. For more information about U-STARS Plus *Science and Literature Connections*, visit http://www.fpg.unc.edu/node/4010

STEM Starters

STEM Starters, a previously funded U.S. Department of Education Jacob K. Javits Act project, developed literacy-focused science curriculum guides to be used with gifted learners.

Blueprints for Biography is a series of teacher curriculum guides with high-level discussion questions, creative and critical-thinking activities, a persuasive writing component, and rich primary resources. STEM *Blueprints* focus on eminent scientists and inventors, including Marie Curie, George Washington Carver, Michael Faraday, and Alexander Graham Bell, for whom exemplary children's biographies exist in trade book form. Each guide concludes with a classic experiment for students to carry out. An innovative peer coaching model specific to science instruction was also developed. For more information about STEM Starters, visit http://ualr.edu/gifted/index.php/home/stem/ at the Jodie Mahony Center for Gifted Education at the University of Arkansas at Little Rock.

Cogito.org

Cogito.org was developed by the Johns Hopkins Center for Talented Youth (CTY), in collaboration with TIP at Duke University, CTD at Northwestern, Rocky Mountain Talent Search at the University of Denver, the Belin-Blank Center at the University of Iowa, C-MITES at Carnegie Mellon, the

Davidson Institute for Talent Development, the Center for Excellence in Education, and Science Service. The goals are to address the needs of gifted students around the world with abilities and interests in math and science. The public site is full of news, interviews with scientists, profiles of young scientists, and a searchable database of programs. Students invited to join as members become part of an online community and participate in discussion forums with each other and with experts in their fields. For more information, visit https://www.cogito.org.

The Davidson Institute for Talent Development
    The Davidson Institute for Talent Development offers links to resources in mathematics, language arts, science, social studies, arts and culture, and related domains. It also provides links to information about educational options such as ability grouping, acceleration, enrichment programs, competitions, and other services. To explore these resources, visit http://www. davidsongifted.org/db/browse_by_topic_resources.aspx

National Science Teachers Association
    The National Science Teachers Association (NSTA) has curricula, assessments, and instructional resources for implementing the NGSS for all students, along with recommendations for a research agenda related to the standards. To access these resources, visit http://www.nsta.org/about/standardsupdate/ resources.aspx.

Neag Center for Gifted Education and Talent Development
    The Neag Center for Gifted Education and Talent Development offers online resources that describe research studies and defensible practices in the field of gifted and talented education. Some of the studies address curriculum at the high school level, the explicit teaching of thinking skills, cluster grouping, algebraic understanding, reading with young children, differentiated performance assessments, and content-based cur-

riculum. To access the studies, visit http://www.gifted.uconn. edu/nrcgt/nrconlin.html.

Colangelo, N., Assouline, S. G., & Gross, M. U. M. (2004). *A nation deceived: How schools hold back America's brightest students.* Iowa City: The University of Iowa, The Connie Belin & Jacqueline N. Blank International Center for Gifted Education and Talent Development.

A Nation Deceived: How Schools Hold Back America's Brightest Students. Templeton National Report on Acceleration by Colangelo et al. (2004) is a two-part report that provides research-based information about acceleration and examines current practices. To download the entire report, visit http://www. accelerationinstitute.org/Nation_Deceived/Get_Report.aspx.

References

Achieve, Inc. (2013a). *Next Generation Science Standards.* Washington, DC: Author.

Achieve, Inc. (2013b). *Three dimensions.* Retrieved from http://www.nextgenscience.org/three-dimensions

Adams, C. (2013). *May the force be with you: Still or moving.* Unpublished lesson for Project Conn-cept.

Benbow, C. P., & Stanley, J. C. (1996). Inequity in equity: How current educational equity policies place able students at risk. *Psychology, Public Policy, and Law, 2,* 249–293.

Brandwein, P. (1988). Science talent: In an ecology of achievement. In P. Brandwein & A. H. Passow, *Gifted young in science: Potential through performance* (pp. 73–103). Washington, DC: National Science Teachers Association.

Breen, M., & Friestad, K. (2008). *The kids' book of weather forecasting.* Nashville, TN: Ideals.

Callahan, C. M., & Kyburg, R. M. (2005). Talented and gifted youth. In D. L. Dubois, & M. J. Karcher (Eds.), *Handbook of youth mentoring* (pp. 424–439). Thousand Oaks, CA: Sage.

Chapin, S. H., O'Connor, C., & Anderson, N. C. (2009). *Classroom discussions: Using math talk to help students learn.* Sausalito, CA: Math Solutions.

Chapman, C. (2009). A smoother acceleration. *The Science Teacher, 76*(3), 42–45.

Cheuk, T. (2012). *Relationships and convergences found in Common Core State Standards in mathematics, Common Core State Standards in ELA/literacy, and a framework for K–12 science education.* Arlington, VA: National Science Teachers Association.

Colangelo, N., Assouline, S. G., & Gross, M. U. M. (2004). *A nation deceived: How schools hold back America's brightest students.* Iowa City: The University of Iowa, The Connie Belin & Jacqueline N. Blank International Center for Gifted Education and Talent Development.

Coleman, M. R., & Shah-Coltane, S. (2010). *U-STARS Plus Science and Literature Connections.* Arlington, VA: Council for Exceptional Children.

Cooney, T. M., Escalada, L. T., & Unruh, R. D. (2008). *PRISMS (Physics Resources and Instructional Strategies for Motivating Students) Plus* [CD version]. Cedar Falls, IA: UNI Physics Department.

Cotabish, A., Dailey, D., Robinson, A., & Hughes, A. (2013). The effects of a STEM intervention on elementary students' science knowledge and skills. *School Science and Mathematics, 113,* 215–226.

Cotabish, A., & Robinson, A. (2012). The effects of peer coaching on the evaluation knowledge, skills, and concerns of gifted program administrators. *Gifted Child Quarterly, 56,* 160–170. doi:10.1177/0016986212446861

Council of Chief State School Officers. (2011). *InTASC model core teaching standards: A resource for state dialogue.* Retrieved from http://www.ccsso.org/resources/programs/interstate_teacher_assessment_consortium_%28intasc%29.html.

Dailey, D., Cotabish, A., & Robinson, A. (2013). A model for STEM talent development: Peer coaching in the elementary classroom. *TEMPO, 1,* 15–19

Feist, G. J. (2006). The development of scientific talent in Westinghouse finalists and members of the National Academy of Sciences. *Journal of Adult Development,13*, 23–35.

Fliegler, L. A. (1961). *Curriculum planning for the gifted.* Englewood Cliffs, NJ: Prentice Hall.

Fowler, M. (1990). The diet cola test. *Science Scope, 13*, 32–34.

Gallagher, S. A., Sher, B. T., Stepien, W. J., & Workman, D. (1995). Implementing problem-based learning in science classrooms. *School Science and Mathematics, 95*, 136-146.

Gardner, H. (1995). Reflections on multiple intelligences: Myths and messages. *Phi Delta Kappan, 77*, 202–209.

Gross, M. U. M. (2006). Exceptionally gifted children: Long-term outcomes of academic acceleration and nonaccelera-tion. *Journal for the Education of the Gifted, 29*, 404–429.

Johnsen, S. K., Kettler, T., & Lord, E. W. (2011, November). *Using the 2010 NAGC pre-K–grade 12 gifted programming standards in professional development.* Paper presented at the annual convention of the National Association for Gifted Children, New Orleans, LA.

Johnsen, S. K., & Sheffield, L. J. (Eds.). (2013). *Using the common core state standards for mathematics with gifted and advanced learners.* Waco, TX: Prufrock Press.

Kitano, M., Montgomery, D., VanTassel-Baska, J., & Johnsen, S. K. (2008). *Using the national gifted education standards for preK-12 professional development.* Thousand Oaks, CA: Corwin Press.

Koscielniak, B. (1998). *Geoffrey groundhog predicts the weather.* Boston, MA: Houghton Mifflin.

Learning Forward. (2011). *Standards for professional learning: Learning communities.* Retrieved from http://www.learningforward.org/standards/learningcommunities/index.cfm

Lieberman, A., & Miller, L. (Eds.). (2008). *Teachers in professional communities.* New York, NY: Teachers College Press.

Little, P. F. B. (2005). Peer coaching as a support to collaborative teaching. *Mentoring and Tutoring, 13*, 83–94.

Maine Mathematics and Science Alliance. (2011). *Earth as a system is essential: Seasons and the seas.* Augusta, ME: MMSA.

Retrieved from http://www.easie-mmsa.org/docs/Data/ DataGraphingLesson.pdf

Melber, L. M. (2003). Partnerships in science learning: Museum outreach and elementary gifted education. *Gifted Child Quarterly, 47,* 251–258.

National Association for Gifted Children. (2004). *NAGC position paper on acceleration.* Retrieved from http://www.nagc.org/ index.aspx?id=383

National Association for Gifted Children. (2008). *The STEM promise: Recognizing and developing talent and expanding opportunities for promising students of science, technology, engineering and mathematics.* Retrieved from http://www.nagc.org/ uploadedFiles/STEM%20white%20paper%281%29.pdf

National Association for Gifted Children. (2010). *NAGC pre-K–grade 12 gifted programming standards: A blueprint for quality gifted education programs.* Washington, DC: Author.

National Association for Gifted Children, & Council for Exceptional Children. (2006). *NAGC-CEC teacher knowledge and skill standards for gifted and talented education.* Retrieved from http://www.nagc.org/NCATEStandards.aspx.

National Research Council. (2012). *A framework for K–12 science education: Practices, crosscutting concepts, and core ideas.* Washington, DC: The National Academies Press.

National Science Board. (2004). *Science and engineering indicators 2004.* Arlington, VA: National Science Foundation. Retrieved from http://www.nsf.gov/statistics/seind04/ pdfstart.htm

National Science Board. (2010). *Preparing the next generation of STEM innovators: Identifying and developing our nation's human capital.* Retrieved from http://www.nsf.gov/nsb/ publications/2010/nsb1033.pdf

National Science Teachers Association. (2011). *NSTA Position statement: Quality science education and 21st-century skills.* Retrieved from http://www.nsta.org/about/ positions/21stcentury.aspx?print=true

Nunn, D. (2012). *Why living things need food*. London, England: Raintree.

Olszewski-Kubilius, P. (2010). Special schools and other options for gifted STEM students. *Roeper Review, 32,* 61–70.

Partnership for 21st Century Skills Framework for 21st Century Learning. (n.d.). *Framework for 21st century learning*. Retrieved from http://www.p21.org/overview.

Robinson, A. (Ed.). (2009-2011). *Blueprint for biography STEM starter series*. Little Rock: University of Arkansas at Little Rock Press.

Sheffield, L. J. (2003). *Extending the challenge in mathematics: Developing mathematical promise in K–8 students*. Thousand Oaks, CA: Corwin Press.

Sheffield, L. J. (2006, March). Developing mathematical promise and creativity. *Journal of the Korea Society of Mathematical Education Series D: Research in Mathematical Education, 10,* 1–11.

Siegle, D., & McCoach, D. B. (2002). Promoting a positive achievement attitude with gifted and talented students. In M. Neihart, S. M. Reis, N. M. Robinson, & S. M. Moon (Eds.), *The social and emotional development of gifted children: What do we know?* (pp. 237–249). Waco, TX: Prufock Press.

Subotnik, R. F., Olszewski-Kubilius, P., & Worrell, F. C. (2012). A proposed direction forward for gifted education based on psychological science, *Gifted Child Quarterly, 56,* 176–188.

Swiatek, M. A., & Benbow, C. P. (1991). A ten-year longitudinal follow-up of ability matched accelerated and unaccelerated gifted students. *Journal of Educational Psychology, 83,* 528–538.

Swiatek, M. A., & Benbow, C. P. (1992). Nonacademic correlates of satisfaction with accelerative programs. *Journal of Youth and Adolescence, 21,* 699–723.

Therrien, W. J., Taylor, J. C., Hosp, J. L., Kaldenberg, E. R., & Gorsh, J. (2011). Science instruction for students with learning disabilities: A meta-analysis. *Learning Disabilities Research and Practice, 26,* 188–203.

VanTassel-Baska, J. L. (Ed.). (2007). *Serving gifted learners beyond the traditional classroom: A guide to alternative programs and services.* Waco, TX: Prufrock Press.

VanTassel-Baska, J., Feng, A., Brown, E., Bracken, B., Stambaugh, T., & French, H. (2008). A study of differentiated instructional change over three years. *Gifted Child Quarterly, 52,* 297–312

Watt, S. J., Therrien, W. J., Kalderberg, E. R. & Taylor, J. (2013). Promoting inclusive practices in inquiry-based science classrooms. *Teaching Exceptional Children, 45,* 40–48.

Wood, S. (2002). Perspectives of best practices for learning gender-inclusive science: Influences of extracurricular science for gifted girls and electrical engineering for women. *Journal of Women and Minorities in Science and Engineering, 8,* 25–40.

Appendix A
Definitions of Key Terms

Acceleration is a broad term used to describe ways in which gifted student learning may occur at a fast and appropriate rate throughout the years of schooling. It refers to content acceleration through preassessment, compacting, and reorganizing curriculum by unit or year, grade skipping, telescoping 2 years into one, dual enrollment in high school and college or university, as well as more personalized approaches such as tutorials, mentorships, and independent research that also would be sensitive to the advanced starting level of these learners for instruction. Both Advanced Placement (AP) and International Baccalaureate (IB) at the high school level represent programs of study already accelerated in content. AP courses also may be taken on a fast-track schedule earlier as appropriate.

Appropriate pacing refers to the rate at which material is taught to advanced learners. Because they are often capable of mastering new material more rapidly than typical learners, appropriate pacing would involve careful preassessment to determine readiness for more advanced material to ensure that advanced learners are not bored with the material and are being adequately challenged. Note that although students might advance quickly through some material, they should also be given time to delve more deeply into topics of interest at appropriate advanced levels of complexity and innovation.

Assessment is the way to determine the scope and degree of learning that has been mastered by the student. For purposes of gifted education, the assessments must be matched to differentiated outcomes, requiring the use of authentic approaches like performance-based and portfolio-based assessment demands. Some assessments are already constructed and available for use, exhibiting strong technical adequacy and employed in research studies, although others may be teacher-developed, with opportunities to establish interrater reliability among teachers who may be using them in schools. Care should be taken to use assessments that do not restrict the level of proficiency that students can demonstrate, such as above-grade-level assessments that allow for innovative and more complex responses.

Characteristics and needs of gifted learners is the basis for differentiating any curriculum area. Scientifically talented learners often have strong spatial skills, see relationships, recognize patterns, make generalizations, and may be highly fluent, flexible, and original at problem finding and scientific inquiry at an earlier stage of development than typical learners. Because of this advanced readiness, these students may need to be accelerated through the basic material in science in order to focus on higher level science concepts and problems.

Complexity refers to a feature of differentiation that provides advanced learners more variables to study, asks them to use multiple resources to solve a problem, or requires them to use multiple higher order skills simultaneously. The degree of complexity may depend on the developmental level of the learner, the nature of the learning task, and the readiness to take on the level of challenge required.

Creativity and innovation are used to suggest that activities used with the gifted employ opportunities for more open-ended project work that mirrors real-world professional work in solving problems in the disciplines. The terms also suggest that advanced learners are proficient in the skills and habits of mind associated with being a creator or innovator in a chosen field of endeavor. Thus, creative thinking and problem-solving skills would be emphasized.

Curriculum is a set of planned learning experiences, delineated from a framework of expectations at the goal or outcome level that represents important knowledge, skills, and concepts to be learned. Differentiated curriculum units of study already have been designed and tested for effectiveness in science, or units may be developed by teachers to use in gifted instruction.

Differentiation of curriculum for gifted learners is the process of adapting and modifying curriculum structures to address these characteristics and needs more optimally. Thus, curriculum goals, outcomes, and activities may be tailored for gifted learners to accommodate their needs. Typically, this process involves the use of the strategies of acceleration, complexity, depth, and creativity in combination.

Instruction is the delivery system for teaching that comprises the deliberate use of models, strategies, and supportive management techniques. For gifted learners, inquiry strategies such as problem-based learning and creative problem solving and problem posing, and critical thinking models such as Paul's Reasoning Model used in independent research or within a flexible grouping approach in the regular classroom constitutes instructional differentiation.

Rigor and relevance suggest that the curriculum experiences planned for advanced learners be sufficiently challenging yet provided in real-world or curricular contexts that matter to learners at their particular stage of development.

Talent trajectory is used to describe the school span development of advanced learners in their area of greatest aptitude from K–16. It is linked to developmental stages from early childhood through adolescence and defines key interventions that aid in the talent development process, specific to the subject area and desired career path.

Teacher quality refers to the movement at all levels of education to improve the knowledge base and skills of classroom teachers at Pre-K–12 levels, which is necessary for effective instruction for advanced students. It is the basis for a redesign of teacher education standards and a rationale for examining Pre-K–12 student outcomes in judging the efficacy of higher education programs for teachers. Policy makers are committed to this issue in improving our Pre-K–16 education programs.

Appendix B
Evidence-Based Practices
in Gifted Education

Evidence-based practices that inform the teacher preparation and programming standards in gifted education relate to assessment, curriculum, instruction, and grouping issues, all of which are embedded within the Next Generation Science Standards. These practices have an extensive research base (*Note*: The full references for the citations below can be found in the research base that accompanies the NAGC-CEC Teacher Preparation Standards in Gifted Education, available on the NAGC website: http://www.nagc.org).

Assessment of Individual Characteristics and Needs

- Because of their advanced cognitive functioning, internal locus of control, motivation, and talents, teachers need to provide intellectual challenge in their classrooms to gifted and talented students (Ablard & Tissot, 1998; Barnett & Durden, 1993; Carter, 1985; Gross, 2000; McLauglin & Saccuzzo, 1997; Robinson & Clinkenbeard, 1998; Swiatek, 1993).

- Educators also must be receptive to gifted students' affective needs and sensitive to the social-emotional and coping needs of special groups of learners such as highly gifted, gifted students with disabilities, gifted students from diverse backgrounds, gifted girls, and gifted boys (Albert & Runco, 1989; Ford & Harris, 2000; Coleman, 2001; Cross, Stewart, & Coleman, 2003; Gross, 2003; Kennedy, 1995; Peterson, 2003; Shaunessy & Self, 1998; Swiatek & Dorr, 1998).
- Gifted students' cultural, linguistic, and intellectual differences should be considered when planning instruction and differentiating curriculum (Boothe & Stanley, 2004).
- Educators need to use preassessment and ongoing assessment to adjust instruction that is consistent with the individual student's progress (Reis, Burns, & Renzulli, 1992; Winebrenner, 2003).
- Assessments used to document academic growth include authentic tasks, portfolios, and rubrics and performance-based assessments (Siegle, 2002; Treffinger, 1994; VanTassel-Baska, 2002; Sheffield, 2003).
- The results of progress assessments can be used to adjust instruction including placement in appropriate group learning settings and academic acceleration (Feldhusen, 1996; Kulik, 1992).

Instruction

- Teachers need to use metacognitive and higher level thinking strategies in the content areas, use activities that address the gifted students' areas of interest, and foster research skills (Anderson & Krathwohl, 2001; Center for Gifted Education, 2000; Elder & Paul, 2003; Hébert, 1993; Johnsen & Goree, 2005; Moon, Feldhusen, & Dillon, 1994; VanTassel-Baska, Avery, Little, & Hughes, 2000).

- Educators should develop gifted students' use of cognitive strategies and encourage deliberate training in specific talent areas (Bloom & Sosniak, 1981; Ericcson & Charness, 1994; Feldman, 2003).
- Technology can be used in independent studies to access mentors and electronic resources and to enroll in advanced classes (Cross, 2004; Ravaglia, Suppes, Stillinger, & Alper, 1995; Siegle, 2004).

Curriculum

- In the classroom, curricular modifications for gifted students include acceleration, enrichment grouping, problem-based learning, curriculum compacting, tiered lessons, independent study, and specific curriculum models (Brody, 2004; Betts & Neihart, 1986; Colangelo, Assouline, & Gross, 2004; Gallagher & Stepien, 1996; Gavin, Casa, Adelson, Carroll, & Sheffield, 2009; Gavin & Sheffield, 2010; Gentry, 1999; Johnsen & Goree, 2005; Kulik & Kulik, 1992; Milgram, Hong, Shavit, & Peled, 1997; Renzulli & Reis, 2004; Rogers, 2003; Southern & Jones, 1991; Tomlinson, 2002; Tomlinson et al., 2001; VanTassel-Baska & Little, 2003).
- Models emphasize the need for considering students' interests, environmental and natural catalysts, curriculum differentiation, and the development of higher level thinking skills (Elder & Paul, 2003; Gagné, 1995; Renzulli & Reis, 2003; Tomlinson & Cunningham-Eidson, 2003).
- When designing a differentiated curriculum, it is essential to develop a scope and sequence and align national, state or provincial, and/or local curricular standards with the differentiated curriculum (Maker, 2004; Tassell, Stobaugh, Fleming, & Harper, 2010; VanTassel-Baska & Johnsen, 2007; VanTassel-Baska & Stambaugh, 2006).

- Specific curricula have been designed for gifted students and include affective education, leadership, domain-specific studies, and the arts (Clark & Zimmerman, 1997; Nugent, 2005; Parker & Begnaud, 2003; VanTassel-Baska, 2003a).
- Educators should integrate academic and career guidance into learning plans for gifted students, particularly those from diverse backgrounds (Cline & Schwartz, 2000; Ford & Harris, 1997).
- Differentiated curricula results in increased student engagement, enhanced reasoning skills, and improved habits of mind (VanTassel-Baska, Avery, Little, & Hughes, 2000).
- When individuals from diverse backgrounds are provided challenging curricula, their abilities and potential are more likely to be recognized (Ford, 1996; Ford & Harris, 1997; Mills, Stork, & Krug, 1992).

Environment

- Working in groups with other gifted students and mentors can yield academic benefits and enhance self-confidence and communication skills (Brody, 1999; Davalos, & Haensly, 1997; Grybe, 1997; Pleiss & Feldhusen, 1995; Torrance, 1984).
- Working under a successful mentor in their areas of interest can foster personal growth, leadership skills, and high levels of learning in gifted students (Betts, 2004; Brody, 1999; Davalos & Haensly, 1997; Feldhusen & Kennedy, 1988; Grybe, 1997; Pleiss & Feldhusen, 1995; Torrance, 1984).
- Other learning situations that support self-efficacy, creativity, and lifelong learning include early college entrance programs, talent searches, science clubs and circles, online and afterschool/summer programs, competitions, problem-based learning, independent play,

independent study, and the International Baccalaureate program (Betts, 2004; Boothe, Sethna, Stanley, & Colgate, 1999; Christophersen & Mortweet, 2003; Gallagher, 1997; Johnsen & Goree, 2005; Karp, 2010; Olszewski-Kubilius, 1998; Poelzer & Feldhusen, 1997; Riley & Karnes, 1998; Rotigel & Lupkowski-Shoplik, 1999; Ruszcyk, 2012; Warshauer et al., 2010).

- Three factors need to be present for students to develop their talents: (a) above-average ability and motivation; (b) school, community, and/or family support; and (c) acceptance by peers in the domain of talent (Bloom, 1985; Csikszentmihalyi, 1996; Gagné, 2003; Renzulli, 1994; Siegle & McCoach, 2005).

Appendix C
Annotated References on Science and Giftedness

Ablard, K. E., Mills, C. J., & Duvall, R. (1994). *Acceleration of CTY math and science students* (Tech. Rep. No. 10). Baltimore, MD: Johns Hopkins University, Center for Talented Youth.

Abstract: Varied types of acceleration, including individually paced precalculus, fast-paced science courses from the Center for Talented Youth, and diagnostic-prescriptive approaches, were examined and student perceptions discussed. Students felt that acceleration was overall positive but felt isolated from their peers and uncomfortable being in classes with older students. However, students felt that the opportunity to be challenged outweighed the social negatives.

Babaeva, J. D. (1999). A dynamic approach to giftedness: Theory and practice. *High Ability Studies, 10,* 51–68.

Abstract: The aims of this research were to investigate the possibilities of developing the cognitive and creative abilities of recognized gifted children and of raising the development of "ordinary" children up to a level of giftedness. This experimental work, based on Vygotsky's Dynamic Theory of Giftedness, involved special procedures and an experimental curriculum designed to overcome children's psychological barriers to learning. Five school classes were involved: three experimental classes, two of which were gifted and one of average-ability children. Two further control classes were taught by conventional methods. Comparative assessments were made for 6 years between all of the children, regarding cognitive development, creativity, and social giftedness, revealing considerable undeveloped potential of "ordinary" children. Major factors influencing IQ changes included the differences in psychological mechanisms to overcome barriers to learning. Due to the experimental psychological curriculum, not only did all of the children's cognitive abilities increase, but also their creativity. Hence, these new diagnostic and developmental procedures were found to be effective, demonstrating the high practical value of the Dynamic Theory of Giftedness.

Brody, L. (2004). *Grouping and acceleration practices in gifted education*. Thousand Oaks, CA: Corwin Press.

Abstract: This volume of seminal articles on grouping and acceleration emphasizes the importance of flexibility when assigning students to instructional groups and modifying the groups when necessary. Grouping and acceleration have proved to be viable tools to differentiate content for students with different learning needs based on cognitive abilities and achievement levels.

Colangelo, N., Assouline, S. G., & Gross, M. U. M. (2004). *A nation deceived: How schools hold back America's brightest students*. Iowa City: The University of Iowa, The Connie Belin & Jacqueline N. Blank International Center for Gifted Education and Talent Development.

Abstract: Interviewed years later, an overwhelming majority of accelerated students say that acceleration was an excellent experience for them. They felt academically challenged and socially accepted, and they did not fall prey to the boredom that plagues many highly capable students who are forced to follow the curriculum for their age-peers. In spite of rich research evidence, schools, parents, and teachers have not accepted the idea of acceleration. *A Nation Deceived* presents the reasons for why schools hold back America's brightest kids, and shows that these reasons are simply not supported by research.

Gross, M. U. M. (2006). Exceptionally gifted children: Long-term outcomes of academic acceleration and non-acceleration. *Journal for the Education of the Gifted, 29,* 40–429.
Abstract: The 20-year longitudinal study traced the academic, social, and emotional development of 60 young Australians with IQs of 160 and above. The 60 youths were spread over Australia with seven living overseas. To be included in the study, the youth needed to be between the ages of 5 and 13 throughout 1988 and 1989. The majority of the children who had been radically accelerated or who were accelerated by 2 years reported high degrees of life satisfaction, have taken research degrees at leading universities, have professional careers, and report facilitative social and romantic relationships. Children of equal abilities who were accelerated by only one year or who were not permitted to accelerate have entered less academically rigorous college courses, reported lower levels of life satisfaction, and experienced significant difficulties with socialization. The author concluded with two primary recommendations. First, students should not only accelerate in their areas of special talent but also be allowed to explore possible pathways of other talent areas. Second, exceptionally gifted students should be identified early and accelerated or placed in a class with other gifted children.

Johnsen, S. (2005). Within-class acceleration. *Gifted Child Today, 28*(1), 5.
Abstract: This article describes ways teachers can accelerate the curriculum in their classrooms by preassessing students and modifying their instruction, allowing them to either move through the curriculum at a faster pace or to provide in-depth learning experiences.

Mills, C. J., & Ablard, K. E. (1993). Credit and placement for academically talented students following special summer courses in math and science. *Journal for the Education of the Gifted, 17,* 4–25

Abstract: The researchers surveyed 892 academically talented students about academic credit and/or course placement for their participation in a precalculus or fast-paced science course during the summer. They found that 39% of the math students received credit and 38% of the science students received credit in their schools.

Olszewski-Kubilius, P., & Yasumoto, J. (1995). Factors affecting the academic choices of academically talented middle school students. *Journal for the Education of the Gifted, 18,* 298–318.

Abstract: Using a sample of 656 middle school students who participated in a summer academic program, these researchers found that gender influences the selection of math and science courses over verbal ones. Parental attitudes, previous educational experiences, and ethnicity (in this study, Asian–American) influenced the selection of math and science courses over verbal courses. The importance that parents place on mathematics and science for their child's future may have the most powerful influence on a child's selection of mathematics and science courses.

Ravaglia, R., Suppes, P., Stillinger, C., & Alper, T. M. (1995). Computer-based mathematics and physics for gifted students. *Gifted Child Quarterly, 39,* 7–13.

Abstract: A group of 27 middle and high school students took computer-based advanced math classes at a middle school. A tutor provided assistance that included correcting offline work, grading tests, and certifying performance in the course. Ninety-two percent of those who took Calculus AB (the first two quarters of college calculus), 100% of those who took Calculus BC (the entire year of college calculus), and 88% of those who took Physics C received scores of 4 or 5 on Advanced Placement tests. The computer courses were designed at the Education Program for Gifted Youth (EPGY) at Stanford University. The authors concluded that computer-based education makes it possible for gifted and talented middle and early high school students to complete advanced courses in mathematics and physics earlier than expected.

Reis, S. M., & Park, S. (2001). Gender differences in high-achieving students in math and science. *Journal for the Education of the Gifted, 25,* 52–73.
Abstract: Using data from the National Education Longitudinal Study of 1988, the researchers examined gender differences between high-achieving students in math and science. They found that there were more high-achieving males than females in this group with far fewer female students in the science group. They also found that high-achieving males felt better about themselves than high-achieving females. Females who are high achieving in math and science are more influenced by teachers and family than males are.

VanTassel-Baska, J. (Ed.). (2004). *Curriculum for gifted and talented students.* Thousand Oaks, CA: Corwin Press.
Abstract: A collection of seminal articles and research from *Gifted Child Quarterly* are compiled in one volume, including how to develop a scope and sequence for the gifted, the Multiple Menu Model of serving gifted students, what effective curriculum for the gifted looks like, curriculum at the secondary level, and specific content area curricula options in math and science.

Vogeli, B. R. (1997). *Special secondary schools for the mathematically and scientifically talented: An international panorama.* New York, NY: Columbia University Teachers College.
Abstract: This is a 284-page report on special schools for the mathematically and scientifically talented. These schools are one manifestation of concern for the identification and development of an important world resource—the gifted youth of every nation. Despite proliferation of special schools, informa-

tion about them is widely dispersed in professional journals, news reports, and advertising literature prepared by the schools themselves. This report, which describes more than 50 special schools in 12 nations, is intended neither as a comparative study nor as an in-depth analysis of individual schools, but rather as an "international guidebook"—a ready reference for those concerned with the education of the gifted. In some schools the curriculum is exemplary, in others the selection process, the facilities, or the faculty are of special interest. Documents of importance, translated into English and appearing as appendices, may be useful in determining differences in curricular emphases, teaching methods, and admission and evaluation standards from school to school. Most foreign documents included have not been previously available in English.

Appendix D
Additional Science Resources

Adams, C. M. (2003). Nurturing talent in science. In P. Olzewski-Kubilius, L. Limburg-Weber, & S. Pfeiffer (Eds.), *Early gifts: Recognizing and nurturing children's talents* (pp. 19–38). Waco, TX: Prufrock Press.

Adams, C. M., & Callahan, C. M. (1995). The reliability and validity of a performance task for evaluating science process skills. *Gifted Child Quarterly, 39*, 14–20.

Adams, C. M., & Pierce, R. L. (2008). Science, Elementary. In J. A. Plucker & C. M. Callahan (Eds.), *Critical issues and practices in gifted education* (pp. 563–578). Waco, TX: Prufrock Press.

Adams, C. M., & Pierce, R. L. (2006). Creative thinking. In F. A. Dixon &, S. M. Moon (Eds). *Handbook of secondary gifted education* (pp. 343–362). Waco, TX: Prufrock Press.

Adams, C. M., & Pierce, R. L. (2003). Teaching by tiering. *Science and Children, 41*, 30–34.

Baram-Tsabari, A., Sethi, R., Bry, L., & Yarden, A. (2006). Using questions sent to an Ask-A-Scientist site to identify children's interests in science. *Science Education, 90*, 1050–1072.

Benbow, C. P., & Minor, L. L. (1986). Mathematically talented students and achievement in the high school sciences. *American Educational Research Journal, 23*, 259–282.

Brandwein, P. (1988). Science talent: In an ecology of achievement. In P. Brandwein, & A. H. Passow, *Gifted young in science: Potential through performance* (pp. 73–103). Washington, DC: National Science Teachers Association.

Callahan, C. M., Adams, C. M., Bland, L. C., Moon, T. R., Moore, S. D., Perie, M. A., & McIntire, J. A. (1996). Factors influencing recruitment, enrollment, and retention of young women in special schools of mathematics, science, and technology. In K. Arnold, K. D. Noble, & R. F. Subotnick (Eds.), *Remarkable women: Perspectives on female talent development* (pp. 243–260). Cresskill, NJ: Hampton Press.

Cooney, T. M., Escalada, L. T., & Unruh, R. D. (2008). *PRISMS (Physics Resources and Instructional Strategies for Motivating Students) Plus* [CD version]. Cedar Falls: University of Northern Iowa Physics Department.

Cooper, C. R., Baum, S. M., & Neu, T. W. (2004). Developing scientific talent in students with special needs: An alternative model for identification, curriculum, and assessment. *Journal of Secondary Gifted Education, 15,* 162–169.

Feng, A. X., VanTassel-Baska, J., Quek, C., Bai, W., & O'Neill, B. (2005). A longitudinal assessment of gifted students' learning using the integrated curriculum model (ICM): Impacts and perceptions of the William and Mary language arts and science curriculum. *Roeper Review, 27,* 78–83.

Gallagher, S. (2012). *An introduction to problem-based learning for classroom teachers.* Unionville, NY: Royal Fireworks Press.

Johnsen, S. K., & Kendrick, J. (Eds.). (2005). *Science education for gifted students.* Waco, TX: Prufrock Press.

Loveless, T., Farkas, S., & Duffet, A. (2008). *High-achieving students in the era of No Child Left Behind: Part 1: An analysis of NAEP data.* Washington, DC: Fordham Institute.

Misset, T. C., Reed, C. B., Scot, T. P., Callahan, C. M., & Slade, M. (2010). Describing learning in an advanced online case-based course in environmental science. *Journal of Advanced Academics, 22,* 10–50.

National Academy of Sciences. (2007). *Rising above the gathering storm: Energizing and employing America for a brighter economic future.* Washington, DC: The National Academies Press.

National Academy of Sciences. (2010). *Rising above the gathering storm, revisited: Rapidly approaching category 5.* Washington, DC: The National Academies Press.

National Center for Education Statistics. (2011). *The nation's report card: Science 2011.* Retrieved from http://nces.ed.gov/nationsreportcard/pdf/main2011/2012465.pdf.

National Research Council. (2002). *Learning and understanding: Improving advanced study of mathematics and science in U.S. high schools.* Washington, DC: The National Academies Press.

National Research Council. (2012). *A framework for K–12 science education: Practices, crosscutting concepts, and core ideas.* Washington, DC: The National Academies Press.

National Science Teachers Association. (2011). *NSTA Position Statement: Quality Science Education and 21st-Century Skills.* Retrieved from http://www.nsta.org/about/positions/21stcentury.aspx?print=true

Olszewski-Kubilius, P. (2010). Special schools and other options for gifted STEM students. *Roeper Review, 32,* 61–70.

Olszewski-Kubilius, P., & Yasumoto, J. (1995). Factors affecting the academic choices of academically talented middle school students. *Journal for the Education of the Gifted, 18,* 298–318.

Renzulli, J. S., Gubbins, J. E., McMillan, K. S., Eckert, R. D., & Little, C. A. (Eds.). (2009). *Systems and models for developing programs for the gifted and talented* (2nd ed.). Waco, TX: Prufrock Press.

Romance, N. R., & Vitale, M. R. (2001). Implementing an in-depth expanded science model in elementary schools: Multi-year findings, research issues, and policy implications. *International Journal of Science Education, 23,* 373–404.

Smith, T., Martin, M., Mullis, I., & Kelly, D. (2000). *The profiles in student achievement in science at the TIMSS international benchmarks.* Chestnut Hill, MA: Boston College, International Study Center, Lynch School of Education.

Stewart, J., Cartier, J., & Passmore, C. (2005). Developing understanding through model-based inquiry. In S. M. Donovan &
J. D. Bransford (Eds.), *How students learn: History, mathematics,
and science in the classroom* (pp. 515–555). Washington, DC:
National Academies Press.

VanTassel-Baska, J. (1999). Science education for gifted and talented children. *The ERIC Review, 6,* 50–51.

VanTassel-Baska, J. (Ed.). (2007). *Serving gifted learners beyond the
traditional classroom: A guide to alternative programs and services.*
Waco, TX: Prufrock Press.

VanTassel-Baska, J., & McFarland, B. (2008). Science, Secondary.
In J. A. Plucker & C. M. Callahan (Eds.), *Critical issues and
practices in gifted education* (pp. 579–594). Waco, TX: Prufrock
Press.

About the Authors

Cheryll M. Adams, Ph.D., is the Director Emerita of the Center for Gifted Studies and Talent Development at Ball State University and teaches online graduate courses in gifted education and elementary education. She has authored or coauthored numerous publications in professional journals, as well as several books and book chapters. She has coauthored and directed three Jacob K. Javits grants. She serves on the editorial review boards for *Roeper Review*, *Gifted Child Quarterly*, *Journal of Advanced Academics*, and *Journal for the Education of the Gifted*. She has served on the Board of Directors of the National Association for Gifted Children and has been president of the Indiana Association for the Gifted and of The Association for the Gifted, Council for Exceptional Children.

Alicia Cotabish, Ed.D., is an assistant professor of teaching and learning at the University of Central Arkansas. Currently, Alicia teaches graduate-level K–12 teacher candidates and secondary science methodology. Alicia directed STEM Starters, a Jacob K. Javits project, and was the former Associate Director of the Jodie Mahony Center for Gifted Education at the University of Arkansas at Little Rock. As a public school teacher, Alicia taught middle school and Pre-AP science, and was an award-winning gifted and talented teacher and coordinator for 8 years in Texas and Arkansas. Her recent work has focused on STEM, gifted education, and peer coaching.

Mary Cay Ricci is the Coordinator of Gifted Education in Baltimore County Public Schools in Maryland. She holds certification in gifted and talented education from Johns Hopkins University, where she is also a faculty associate in the Graduate School of Education Gifted Certification Program. Mary Cay has coauthored several articles for *Parenting for High Potential*. Her book, *Mindsets in the Classroom: Building a Culture of Success and Student Achievement in Schools* will be released in September 2013.